"For all of us who have been trained to re... it immediately about us and what we're supp...u to do, Elyse introduces us to a much better way—the way Jesus taught his followers to read and understand it, which puts who he is and what he's done firmly at the center of every part of the Bible's story."

"Whether you have studied the Bible for years or just begun, *Finding the Love of Jesus from Genesis to Revelation* will renew your mind and refresh your soul. In her engaging style, Elyse makes deep truths understandable as she teaches us how to see Jesus in all of Scripture."

"They say that 'context is king' in understanding Scripture, and certainly daughters of the King have a right to know. I love that Elyse's new book is laser-focused on helping us see the context of God's big story and how all the pieces fit together."

"I love it when a writer explains deep truths in a relatable way. Elyse has written a seminary-level overview of the whole story of Scripture, but she has made it accessible to the average man or woman who may feel seminary is out of their league. Churches need more resources like this."

"With a gentle hand and clear eye, Fitzpatrick guides readers to discover a loving God within the pages of Scripture. But not just any God. Fitzpatrick reveals a purposeful, active God who offers life and hope through the gospel—a God who has loved us from the very start."

"In a clear and concise manner, Elyse demonstrates how to approach the Scriptures as Jesus did: 'Beginning with Moses and all the Prophets, he interpreted to them in all the Scriptures the things concerning himself' (Luke 24:27). Elyse offers a much-needed corrective to the self-oriented approach to Bible study so prevalent today."

—Lydia Brownback, author and speaker

"Elyse is someone I've always counted on to point me to Jesus in every sentence she writes and in every word she speaks. In her latest book, and best work yet, Elyse does it again. This book was written for the woman who wonders if her life is of any worth to Jesus, and the woman who worries that she isn't welcome in his presence, and the woman who wants to know what Jesus wants for her. So basically, it's for all of us! *Finding the Love of Jesus from Genesis to Revelation* is an irresistible invitation to learn, from a wise and skilled teacher, about the Jesus who loves you and longs to open your eyes to who he is, and who you are in him."

—Jeannie Cunnion, author of *Mom Set Free*

"*Does Jesus really love me?* If that's your question, let Elyse take you by the hand and show you, opening door after door in the Scriptures with the key given by Jesus himself. See his love and then learn to find it for yourself. *Yes, Jesus loves me!*"

—Rondi Lauterbach, author of *Hungry: Learning to Feed Your Soul with Christ*

"Elyse has orchestrated a beautiful yet practical resource for those who long to understand how each biblical story, letter, prophecy, and poem fits into the whole counsel of Scripture. From Genesis to Revelation, this book will teach you how to read any and every verse through the interpretive lens of the Gospel. Grab this book, read it through immediately, then keep it on your shelf as a reference to carefully savor for years to come."

—Katie Orr, Bible teacher and creator of the FOCUSed15 Bible studies

"Elyse's no-nonsense writing style and accessible approach to Scripture give her books the flavor of a long-overdue conversation with a trusted friend. Even better, reading her book only stokes my desire to read The Book, and for that I am most grateful."

—Amanda Bible Williams, author and chief content officer at She Reads Truth

◆

FINDING
THE
LOVE
OF
JESUS

◆

from
Genesis
to
Revelation

◆

Books by Elyse Fitzpatrick

FROM BETHANY HOUSE PUBLISHERS

Home

Answering Your Kids' Toughest Questions*

*Finding the Love of Jesus from
Genesis to Revelation*

*with Jessica Thompson

FINDING
THE
LOVE
OF
JESUS

from
Genesis
to
Revelation

ELYSE FITZPATRICK

BETHANYHOUSE
a division of Baker Publishing Group
Minneapolis, Minnesota

© 2018 by Elyse Fitzpatrick

Published by Bethany House Publishers
11400 Hampshire Avenue South
Bloomington, Minnesota 55438
www.bethanyhouse.com

Bethany House Publishers is a division of
Baker Publishing Group, Grand Rapids, Michigan

Printed in the United States of America

ISBN 978-0-7642-1801-9

Library of Congress Control Number: 2017961363

Cover design by Rob Williams, InsideOutCreativeArts

18 19 20 21 22 23 24   7 6 5 4 3 2 1

To every woman who has ever wondered
whether the Son could love her or would
want to be near her . . .
because, after all, she isn't a man.

Contents

Acknowledgments

I'm so thankful for the many women and men who have poured into my life and faith through the years. From the very beginning of my Christian walk, I've been the recipient of theological teaching and never was told that theology wasn't for women. I'm so thankful for that!

I'm thankful for George and Rita Evans, Doug and Val Balcombe, Dave and Darlene Eby, Craig and Ginger Cabaniss, Mark and Rondi Lauterbach, Iain and Barb Duguid, and many, many others who pressed me into Scripture and the Scripture into me.

And, as always, special thanks go to Scott Lindsey and my friends at FaithLife/Logos for developing Bible software that make it easy for me to look like I'm smarter than I am. You guys are the best!

I'm thankful for my pastors and their wives at Valley Center Community Church who have prayed faithfully for me.

I'm also grateful for my friends, Julie, Anita, and Donna, and for my wonderful family and their kiddos.

And, of course, I'm thankful for my dear husband, Phil, who never once told me that I shouldn't study and learn and love the Lord because I was "just a girl."

Thanks also to my friends at Bethany House, especially Andy McGuire.

Introduction

Forever and Forever He Has Loved Us

Jesus loves women. He has loved us since the beginning, even from before the words *"in the beginning . . ."* were written. Think of it, even "before the ages began"[1] he loved us and made a way for us to know and love him in return. He specifically created us as women for he loves our womanness and longed for us to know his love. As part of the Trinity—the Father, Son, and Spirit—God the Son expressed love for women during all the Old Testament times, even though his incarnation as the Man, Christ Jesus, was thousands of years in the future. Before Bethlehem he loved us. And he has promised to love us until the end, when we will finally be beautified as his bride and will celebrate his love forever. Jesus has always loved women. He always will.[2]

Jesus' love for women was costly. During his earthly ministry he was scorned because of it. He was a man who crossed over lines of proper decorum to express his love for women. Because he was a pious Jew, he was expected to keep women—especially women of a certain sort—at arm's length. Instead, he shocked his disciples by befriending a five-times-married, immoral half-breed (John 4:7–27). He welcomed the kisses of a woman of questionable morals and was scorned for it by Simon, a Pharisee, who concluded that Jesus couldn't possibly be a prophet because he wouldn't have let a woman like that touch him had he known what she was (Luke 7:38–39).

He was derided by the religious elite, who "grumbled" about him because he received sinners and ate with them (Luke 15:2). Then he healed a woman whose menstrual blood had made her religiously unclean and had kept her from knowing any human touch for twelve years. Twelve years! He knew that to touch her would make him ceremonially unclean, and so did everyone else. When she tried to hide from him in shame, he insisted that she come forward and receive his love. He lovingly called her his "daughter" (Luke 8:42–48). He spoke peace into her troubled soul. How long had it been since she'd heard words of kindness from a man? Immediately after that encounter, he went into the home of a religious leader whose little daughter had just died. He touched her lifeless hand, again breaking the law, and said, "Child, arise" (Luke 8:49–56). His love for women drove him to open his arms and heart to the outcast, the immoral, the unclean, and the dead. He loved and received their touch, moved by compassion.

Jesus loved women, and because he loved them, he loved opening their hearts to the truth of who he was. It was his joy. He taught them about his eternal love for them and who they would become because of him. He taught them that his love was strong enough to overcome all their sin and fear and confusion. He told them that his love would lead him up Golgotha's mount to a gruesome execution, where they would weep (Luke 24:6–7), so that he could rescue them from sin and death. And he wanted them to know that his love would pull him back from death's maw and into a garden where he would once again speak to a woman he loved, which was why he told them he would rise again. God touched them. They touched God.

Engaging women in conversation was normal for the Lord. They were welcomed into the inner circle of his followers (Luke 8:1–3) and he freely allowed them to hear his teaching. Rather than restricting them to conventional domestic roles, he chided busy Martha and told her that her sister Mary had chosen the *one* necessary activity when she shunned her kitchen duties to sit at his feet and learn from him (Luke 10:41–42). Jesus loved the fact that Mary wanted to learn so he stoked that fire within her. Women were invited to listen to him. God spoke words to them.

Then, not long afterward, he taught another woman named Mary (Magdalene) on the morning of his resurrection. Perhaps to make a point about how much he loved being with women, he arranged it so that a woman would be the first human being to hear his voice at his resurrection. In the twenty-first-century Western world in which I live, it's easy to miss the significance of this event. I'm accustomed to seeing women welcomed into important conversations and as lawful witnesses in a courtroom, but that is very different from how it was in first-century Israel. His meeting her *first* was shocking. In this instance, he didn't just cross over a line. He obliterated it. Think of it: Jesus chose a *woman* to be the one who would hear the first word uttered in the new world. And what was that first word? *A woman's name: Mary.* Her response? *Rabboni!* Although Jesus was frequently referred to as *Rabbi* or *Teacher*, this is the only use of *Rabboni* in the New Testament. It's a very special title, a term of endearment, almost like a nickname. It expresses a deeper meaning than simply *Teacher*, though it does mean that. It denotes profound respect and affection or nearness[3] (John 20:16). In essence, she called him *my dear Friend, my beloved Teacher, my Bestie.* When Jesus spoke her name, she responded immediately with her favorite appellation of him: *Rabboni!* Think of it—what came to Mary's mind when she realized that Jesus had risen from the dead wasn't *Jeshua,* his proper name, or *Lord,* or even *Rabbi,* but rather *beloved Teacher.* He had been many things to Mary, but he was primarily her Teacher. So she greeted him as her *Rabboni, best Friend, beloved Teacher.* How did her beloved Teacher respond? He taught her about his ongoing mission (John 20:17). Jesus' meeting with Mary in the garden wasn't a fluke. It was a preordained event between a beloved Teacher—Mary's Rabboni—and his beloved student, and it's meant to tell us something: He wants women to share in his love and mission. A woman was commissioned by God to spread the good news.

With whom did Jesus speak next? Two disciples (Luke 24:13), whom we can safely assume are his uncle Cleopas (Luke 24:18) and another disciple, probably Cleopas' wife, who was Jesus' aunt Mary.[4] I know that might be a bit of a surprise to you, especially if you've seen any of the artwork that depicts Jesus walking down the road with two men. It's easy to assume that the two disciples Jesus intercepted were men, but there is no reason (aside from tradition) to do so. One of them is clearly identified as Cleopas in Luke's account. At another place, John writes that Cleopas' wife, whose name was Mary, had been in Jerusalem, standing with Jesus' mother and his dear friend Mary Magdalene, at the foot of the cross. Wouldn't it make sense then to conclude that after the crucifixion, when all their hope was gone, when they were completely disheartened and bewildered, that they would decide to return home together to try to rebuild their lives after Friday's tragic events?[5]

In this, his second appearance on Easter Sunday, Jesus was delighted to talk with and teach another beloved woman. His conversation with her mirrored the important dialogue he had had with Mary Magdalene. He wasn't simply speaking sentimental words to cheer up his aunt after what had to have been a most heartbreaking weekend in Jerusalem. No, he taught her and her husband deep truths about himself, and especially about how he was the focus of all the Old Testament Scriptures. Mary was certainly acquainted with the prophecies that foretold the coming Messiah, and she undoubtedly had experienced Jesus' welcoming love, but she hadn't yet put those two truths together. She hadn't yet seen how he filled the pages of the Scriptures long before he occupied a manger in Bethlehem. The Lord knew that Mary needed to see him in his fullness, so he became her Rabboni, too. Everything that his aunt thought she understood about what the Law, the Psalms, and the Prophets taught was turned on its head in a few short hours. God taught a woman how to interpret the Scriptures.

The significance of this conversation (and the ones he eventually had with the rest of the disciples) cannot be overstated. This Emmaus road dialogue changed the way the earliest Christians understood the Bible. It shaped how they wrote the New Testament, and it should change and shape us, too. Their new understanding of the Old Testament Scriptures transformed them from ambitious cowards to bold martyrs for the truth. It enabled Mary, and women everywhere, to rightly understand not only what had just happened in Jerusalem but also how those events were part of God's sovereign plan, a plan that would eventually affect women everywhere. He spoke this monumental truth to a man *and* a woman. Both genders needed to hear that the old way of doing religion was over.

Jesus may have lived at a time when training in the Scriptures was primarily a male endeavor, but he continuously let women know that learning about him was something that he not only offered to them but also expected from them. He loved teaching women, and they loved learning from him. He honored them as valued daughters with the God-given ability to reason and learn and who were not only invited into his classroom but also had the capacity to grasp deep truth. He wanted them there. More than that, he expected them to be there.

You Are Welcome at Rabboni's School, Too

Jesus never changes. His love for women hasn't waned. He loves teaching women and he rejoices when they sit down with their Bibles open and ask him to open their minds and hearts. He's just as pleased to teach you as he was to teach them, regardless of your background, ability, or opportunities.

Think about it: These three Marys were very different women. Mary of Bethany was a single woman who lived with her siblings, Martha and Lazarus. Mary Magdalene was probably also single and was a woman from whom Jesus had cast out demons. Perhaps she was independently wealthy, as she is mentioned as one of several women who supported Jesus out of her "means" (Luke 8:1–3). Jesus' aunt Mary had married into his family and was the mother of two sons (Mark 15:40). Two single women and one married mom were called into the role of beloved pupil and disciple.

Jesus loves women: He loves their minds and their hearts, and he loves to teach them so that they'll grow in their understanding of who he is and all he has done. We, too, can be assured of our growth because Jesus knows us. He knows our capacities and he also knows what he can enable us to do. Jesus is our Rabboni, our sweet Master Teacher, and he will teach us all that we need to learn as we spend time looking into that paradigm-shattering conversation Jesus had with his aunt and uncle on the Emmaus road. Let's pray that he will open our minds to understand truth so that we can say, along with his aunt Mary, "Did not our hearts burn within us . . . while he opened to us the Scriptures?" (Luke 24:32). Have you ever felt that way? Wouldn't you like to?

Walking to Emmaus with Our Bestie

So now, I invite you, in the name of the Rabboni who loves to teach women, into this study. I promise to keep it doable, though I will be pressing you to think and work through brief questions at the end of each chapter.

Because we are going to spend the rest of this book studying the lessons that Jesus began to teach on that first Easter Sunday, I won't belabor them now. But there is one last thought I would like to leave with you: *We can't understand the Lord's Word without his enlightening presence.* We need him to open our minds to truth. "Then he *opened* their [the disciples'] minds to understand the Scriptures" (Luke 24:45). In other words, if he doesn't work by his Spirit while we read and pray and search for light, then the Word he wrote will remain unclear, connections between the Old and the New Testaments will be hazy, and we'll fall prey to the fallacy that the Bible is primarily about us and our lives. On the other hand, we may become apathetic about reading it because we will have concluded (even if we don't give voice to this sentiment) that the Bible doesn't really apply to our daily lives . . . at least not the way that blogs, social media, or other books do. And even more tragically, either way we will miss the main point, the ultimate story of the ages: Jesus' saving love for women and for all people.

So pray with me now that the Spirit of Christ, your Teacher, would begin to furnish you with new eyes to see Jesus' story in all the Scriptures. We know his story is there because he said it was. But in the same way that his aunt Mary needed help to see him, we need that help, too. You might start by praying something like this:

My Father in heaven, I want to learn to see your Beloved Son, Jesus, in the Word you've given me. Please send your Spirit to open my eyes and help me as I learn this new way to understand what you've said. And please fill my heart with hope that I can do this because you love to bless your daughters with portrayals of your Son. I'm praying in the name of Jesus. Amen.

I promise you that I am praying for you and for all who are reading this book, that your hearts will be filled with zeal as you see the grandeur of the ageless story of the Redeemer who loves you.

Jesus' aunt Mary testified that her talk with him on the Emmaus road opened her heart and set her on fire. And that, my sisters, is what I'm hoping you'll say when you get to the end of our time together. I hope you'll say that he has opened the Scriptures to you and that your heart has been set ablaze as you gaze on the Savior, the subject of the Bible, the One who has loved you from Genesis to Revelation.

Jesus loves women, and because he loves them, he loves to teach them. He's your Rabboni, your beloved Teacher, your Bestie, and he wants to help you to see him, and to see yourself as part of his story. You are welcome here.

1

It's All about Him

"Did not our hearts burn within us while he talked to
us on the road, while he opened to us the Scriptures?"

Luke 24:32

Sure, I Believe in the Bible, But . . .

I'm so glad you're here. I'm glad that you've chosen to spend time
listening for Jesus to speak his love for you through opening the
Scriptures to you. I'm glad because I know that when he opens
up your heart and mind, when he talks with you on your journey,
you'll be transformed. You'll move from disillusionment, apathy,
and confusion, to zeal, comfort, and joy.

But let's get really honest first: How long has it been since you
felt a passion or excitement about spending time in the Word?
Sure, you read the Bible, but when it's time to read the Bible,

do you anticipate that Jesus will feed you, or has Bible reading become a guilt-motivated duty? If that's what it has become to you, you'll struggle to get it done. And if spending time in the Bible is not something you do as much as you think you should, you wouldn't be alone. A recent Barna Research Group study found that although a majority of Americans hold a high view of the Scriptures, only slightly more than "one-third reads it once a week or more."[1]

Why don't we read the Bible more? Sure, there are plenty of shiny things to distract us, not the least of which is social media. And it's also true that we are all really busy with home and family and work, but still, if we say that we believe the Bible is truly God's Word, why don't we make reading it a priority? *Could it be that we're disconnected from it because it seems so disconnected from us?* After all, what do those strange laws about blood sacrifices or odd predictions of doom have to do with getting the kids to ballet or baseball practice, or even the Christianity we've embraced? Could it be that the Bible, especially the Old Testament, seems pretty much irrelevant to our faith, maybe even a contradiction to the story of Jesus we've embraced? In addition, could it be that we're expecting the Bible to do or be something for us that was never intended? Is it possible we're not reading it like it was meant to be read? If so, we're not alone; even Jesus' disciples were mistaken, and their misunderstanding caused both confusion and discouragement.

Let's listen in now to the conversation Jesus had with his aunt Mary and uncle Cleopas on that first Easter Sunday. Here is Luke's account:

That very day two of them were going to a village named Emmaus, about seven miles from Jerusalem, and they were talking with each other about all these things that had happened. While they were talking and discussing together, Jesus himself drew near and went with them. But their eyes were kept from recognizing him. And he said to them, "What is this conversation that you are holding with each other as you walk?" And they stood still, looking sad. Then one of them, named Cleopas, answered him, "Are you the only visitor to Jerusalem who does not know the things that have happened there in these days?" And he said to them, "What things?" And they said to him, "Concerning Jesus of Nazareth, a man who was a prophet mighty in deed and word before God and all the people, and how our chief priests and rulers delivered him up to be condemned to death, and crucified him. But we had hoped that he was the one to redeem Israel. Yes, and besides all this, it is now the third day since these things happened. Moreover, some women of our company amazed us. They were at the tomb early in the morning, and when they did not find his body, they came back saying that they had even seen a vision of angels, who said that he was alive. Some of those who were with us went to the tomb and found it just as the women had said, but him they did not see. And he said to them, "O foolish ones, and slow of heart to believe all that the prophets have spoken! Was it not necessary that the Christ should suffer these things and enter into his glory?" And beginning with Moses and all the Prophets, he interpreted to them in all the Scriptures the things concerning himself.

Luke 24:13–27

Imagine the scene: Mary, Cleopas' wife, had been one of the women who had been with Jesus in his ministry (Mark 15:40–41). Then she had stood with his mother Mary and Mary Magdalene to witness his execution (John 19:25). After the guards had taken his body down, she and her husband wept the Sabbath day away before leaving Jerusalem on Easter Sunday, brokenhearted and disillusioned. Like other married couples, they probably talked out their grief, trying to process what they had just experienced. This must have been a fairly intense conversation because they didn't stop when a stranger joined them. "What are you talking about?" asked the stranger, who was actually the Lord. Assuming that he must have overheard some of their conversation, Cleopas responded, "Are you the only one in Jerusalem who hasn't heard what has happened during the last few days?" The stranger pressed them, "What things?"

Listen carefully now to Cleopas' response and see if you can picture yourself responding as they did. He said, "We had hoped he would. . ." It is in this part of the dialogue that we learn about the mistaken assumptions Cleopas (and all of the disciples) held. They had rightly recognized Jesus as a great prophet. They had heard him speak, they had seen his miracles. But they had also hoped that he was their Messiah, the One who would redeem Israel.

In order to understand their hopelessness, we need to see what kind of redemption they were expecting. Usually when Christians use the word *redemption*, they mean "freedom from sin" or "the gift of salvation." But that's not what these disciples were expecting. They were expecting national liberation. They thought Jesus would free them from the rule of the Romans.[2] But on that Friday, instead of being freed from the oppression of Rome, they watched as their "Deliverer" was condemned to death. Every hope of liberation from oppression was drowned beneath the blood-soaked ground of Golgotha. All of their assumptions had been wrong, and because of that they were miserable. The Scriptures no longer made sense to them. Of course they were "sad" (Luke 24:17).

Can you see how their misunderstanding of the Old Testament eventuated in grief and hopelessness? It had been from those

Scriptures that they had learned about the Messiah's redemption of Israel. Were the Scriptures false? Could God's Word be trusted?

But they were not only grieving and hopeless. They were also confused. Their confusion stemmed from the fact that some of the women testified that Jesus was actually alive. Even though he had foretold his resurrection on numerous occasions,[3] his closest friends were completely dumbfounded. They didn't believe the women's report. Why? Because they held false assumptions. They completely misunderstood the Scriptures. Their faulty beliefs stopped them from hearing his words about his encroaching death, so of course they weren't comforted by his assurances of his resurrection. They had filtered all his words through their mistaken assumptions. They were shocked by his death, though he had foretold it numerous times. They were confused and doubtful about the resurrection, even when their friends testified to it. How could they have been so blind to Jesus' plan? Because they had willfully misread the Scriptures, they were foolish and unbelieving. From Genesis to Malachi they had gotten the entire Old Testament all wrong.

Learning a New Way to Read

It is easy to ask how they could have been so mistaken as to miss his clear teaching—and yet, we're very much like them. We think we know God's plans, the ways he works, the promises he's made, and then we find ourselves wandering down our own personal Emmaus road, wondering where we took a wrong turn, or if the Bible is even true at all. Like them, we're prone to misread the Scriptures.

Like us, even Jesus' closest friends had failed to understand that there was something, or rather *Someone*, who connected all the law, histories, poems, and prophecies into one basic story, a story that was meant to give them hope and build their faith. Though they were steeped in the teachings of Moses, the Psalms, and the Prophets, they didn't know that the Scriptures weren't meant to show them how to *earn* God's favor, eternal life, or worldly success. Even though they loved him, they failed to see that the Scriptures were about Jesus and how *he* would earn God's favor for them. Of course they were grieving and confused. They were blind to their only source of hope.

With typical patience and love for his miserable friends, Jesus began his teaching at the beginning with the writings of Moses, and then worked his way through to "all the Prophets." He interpreted "to them in all the Scriptures the things concerning himself" (Luke 24:27). But he didn't just reveal truth from the Pentateuch (the first five books of the Bible), or the Prophets (the last seventeen books of the Old Testament). These terms meant *all* the Old Testament Scriptures, for all the "patterns of God's activity again and again throughout the Old Testament looked forward to Jesus himself."[4]

Think about that. Jesus, a man who had read the Hebrew Scriptures from the time he was a child, interpreted the underlying meaning of everything he read as being about himself. That's a shockingly narcissistic thing to do. We would be right to question the reliability of such a statement—if the person who uttered it hadn't just risen from the dead. Mary and Cleopas had seen him die and now they heard his voice. Because Jesus rose from the dead, we can trust that his words are true: the entire Old Testament, from Genesis to Malachi, is his story, the story of his rescue mission of his beloved bride. It *is* all about him.

Mary and Cleopas weren't unique in misreading the Scriptures. Even his closest friends had wrongly assumed it presented the way to *earn* eternal life and reestablish their nation as a world leader. But that wasn't Moses' or the prophets' message at all (John 5:39). Neither they nor their personal success were the theme of those ancient writings. *Jesus was.* He said, "If you believed Moses, you would believe me; for he wrote of me" (John 5:46).

Right about now you might be thinking: *Hold on a minute, Elyse! How could Jesus say that Moses wrote about him? Jesus hadn't yet been born when Moses wrote! How could he say that the Scriptures were all about him?* I understand that objection, and we'll spend the rest of this book answering it more fully, but for now let me just propose this: On that first Easter, in the first Sunday school, Jesus called his listeners (and us) to a new way of understanding his Word. In essence, he taught this one lesson:

> You've been reading the Scriptures all wrong. You thought they were about you and your earthly glory and freedom from suffering. But they are actually about me: my suffering and my eventual glory. Every part of the Bible is all about me.

It would bring great relief to us if we consistently understood the Bible the way Jesus taught this little class to do. But like them, we misread the main message of the Bible. The Bible isn't about us. It isn't even primarily about God in a generic sense—though, of course, it does reveal the Trinity. Rather, it especially highlights the person and work of God the Son, Jesus Christ. Everything that's in there is there for one reason: It points to Jesus—who he is, what he's done, and our need for him, accomplished through his suffering and glory by the will of the Father and the power of the Spirit.

As I said, Jesus spent his entire life studying Moses' writings. He alone knew the true meaning of the Torah. He alone understood that Moses had been writing about him. But he also knew that it wouldn't be until after his death and resurrection, when he walked among his family and friends and taught them again, that they would finally be willing to accept the truth about who he really is. So he patiently waited to teach them while they continued in their grief and confusion.

Welcome to Rabboni's Sunday School

Like those early disciples, we need help if we're going to see how God's Word (from both the Old and New Testaments) connects with our lives. We need to learn what the Bible is actually about and how its truth intersects with our struggle to live by faith today. We need to find answers to these questions:

- Is there one unifying story that binds all the other stories, poems, and prophecies together—not only with events during Jesus' life but also with my life in the here-and-now?

- How are the ancient histories, written thousands of years ago, thousands of miles from where I live, relevant to my life and belief in a post-Christian nation like America?

- Are the song lyrics that fill the Psalms or the wise words penned by Solomon in Proverbs actually meant to speak to me about my Savior and the life he's called me to live?

- Should I read the stories about the "heroes" of the Old Testament and conclude that I'm supposed to be like them? Are their stories put there to teach me a moral lesson, a kind of spiritual *Aesop's Fables*? Should I seek to emulate their lifestyle and then expect the same results they experienced?

To answer these questions, we need to read the Bible the way it was meant to be read—*as one big love story.* Though it contains sixty-six different books written over hundreds of years, the Bible is actually just one long love letter written from our Lord to us, his bride. We need to read it the way Jesus did: as *his* story. It is the story of his loving creation of a world that would tragically fall into rebellion and then be magnificently redeemed through his work on the cross, all to the praise of his glorious grace.

What He Taught Them

So starting with the books that Moses wrote, Jesus went through to the Prophets and "interpreted to them in all the Scriptures the things concerning himself" (Luke 24:27). In one afternoon's stroll, Mary and Cleopas had their eyes opened to the fact that the Messiah was, in fact, right there throughout all the Scriptures they had studied all their lives. They were finally ready to hear his message. They came to it now in humility and with broken hearts, as people who had lost everything and who knew they didn't have answers or any hope of political liberation. And that's just the place they needed to be. They would never have been willing to hear it otherwise.

Are you ready, maybe even longing, to hear his message now? In the chapters to come, we'll discover Jesus in the writings of Moses. We'll see him in the historical narratives about the nation of Israel, and in the song lyrics that David (and others) penned about the Good Shepherd. We'll see him standing before us in all the prophecies—those that obviously speak about a coming Messiah, but also in those that seem not to. We'll learn what makes the Bible a vibrant story of love, rescue, and true redemption. And we'll see Jesus standing there with us, continually reorienting our hearts toward him. Once we begin to see him like this, our hearts will burn with zeal, too, and perhaps we'll actually look forward to reading the Word again, because we know that when we do, we'll find him there: the Lover of our souls.

One Woman with Eyes to See

We've spent a lot of time in this chapter talking about the disillusionment, confusion, and apathy Jesus' disciples (and we) suffer. We've seen that Jesus loved to teach truth, especially to women, and that without the reorientation he brought we will always try to make the Bible about us instead of about him. And that perspective will cause us to struggle to even want to read his Word.

There was, however, one woman who understood his message of suffering *before* glory. We read about her in John 12: "Mary therefore took a pound of expensive ointment made from pure nard, and anointed the feet of Jesus and wiped his feet with her hair" (v. 3).

While Martha was busy preparing dinner and the other disciples sat around waiting to eat it, one person, a woman, Mary of Bethany, anointed him with a precious perfume. Judas, the greedy glory hog, rebuked her for wasting money. But Jesus came to her defense. "Let her alone," he chided. "She's anticipating and honoring the day of my burial" (John 12:7 THE MESSAGE). While everyone else was focused on getting dinner (and plotting their great success), Mary was at his feet, loving him, worshiping him, and preparing his body for his burial. Perhaps she sensed what was about to happen. Maybe his message of suffering before glory had found a niche in her heart because she was a woman who didn't have anything left to lose. She was single and childless. She was wholly dependent upon the care of her brother Lazarus, whom she had already buried once. She knew her position was precarious.

Maybe she understood Jesus' message of suffering before glory in ways that others couldn't, learning it during those dark days when Lazarus lay dying and her beloved Teacher ignored her. She had lived through days of tears and despair, concluding that all was lost. But she had also tasted glory when her despair turned into joy, as Jesus cried, "Lazarus, come out" (John 11:43). Mary learned then that suffering came before glory. She had lived it, and she knew that she would soon live it again in his death. Even though she believed in Jesus' ultimate resurrection in eternity, she went with spices on Easter to cover the odor of his decaying body. But on that morning she would be astounded by glory.

For a second time, we see the Lord defending his dear student, follower, and friend. Jesus never rebuked a woman who loved him, who loved to learn from him, who expressed love for him. He won't rebuke you, either.

Perhaps as you come to him now you can confess to belonging to that group of believing women who rarely read the Bible. Maybe you've sadly admitted that though you love Jesus and believe his Word is good, you haven't been able to make the connection between it and the life you're living. Perhaps you're beginning to see that you've missed the main point, the big picture that Jesus spoke of. Maybe that's because you've wanted to arrange your life the way you've dreamt it would be and you've looked to the Bible to help you do that. Or maybe it's simply because you've never heard that every part of the Bible is actually about him.

In the pages that follow, we'll consider Jesus' words from Luke 24 more closely and make connections from them to our lives and to the faith we love. In the meantime, though, let me encourage you not only to answer the questions below but also to pray that your heart and mind would be opened to see that the whole Bible testifies of him.

OPEN BIBLE, OPEN HEART

1. Do you believe the Bible is actually God's Word? Why or why not?

2. Honestly consider how much time you spend reading the Bible. If you don't read it regularly, are you able to identify the reasons why you don't? Does it seem disconnected or confusing? Are there other things that distract you or seem more important?

3. Have you ever read the Old Testament? What did you think of it? (Be honest!)

4. Spend time in prayer now, asking the Lord to open your heart and mind to truth.

5. In four or five sentences, summarize what you've learned in this chapter.

_____

_____

_____

For Further Study

1. After rereading Luke 24:13–27, answer the following questions:

    • What's the setting for this story (time/place)?

    _____

    _____

    • Who are the main characters?

    _____

    _____

    • Are there any secondary characters?

    _____

    _____

    • What do the main characters say?

    _____

    _____

    • Summarize Cleopas' confession of disappointment, disillusionment, and confusion. (Hint: "We had hoped he was . . ." and "Some of the women . . .")

    _____

    _____

    _____

- Summarize Jesus' teaching in response.

- How did Jesus characterize these disciples' misunderstanding?

- What did he say their problem was?

- Can you identify the primary point of Jesus' teaching in this passage? If so, what is it?

2. Jesus said Moses wrote of him. What do you think he meant? Can you think of any place where he did? (Help: Deuteronomy 18:15)

3. Jesus talked about suffering before glory—something that Mary of Bethany likely understood. Is that your understanding of the Bible's message? Why or why not?

2

Seeing What's Right before You

Then he opened their minds to understand the Scriptures.

Luke 24:45

Smog is ubiquitous in Southern California. Though I live in San Diego, where we rarely choke on the foul stuff, I do travel to Los Angeles frequently enough to recognize the "smog headache," burning eyes, and constricted breathing that is part of our northerly trip up the I-5. After a few moments, though, I do tend to acclimate to it and am no longer so aware of it. In fact, I don't even think about it, unless I'm driving down into the Los Angeles basin from the San Gabriel Mountains, and I can see a brown haze hanging over the whole city. I think, *How on earth can anyone breathe that stuff?* Yet, and here's the strange thing, when I'm walking around breathing that in, I can't see it. Sure, my eyes might burn a little, but I can't see it at all. Air just seems like, well, air.

Like breathing smog in Southern California, it's nearly impossible to be aware of things that are just part of our daily environment. I've heard people say, "A fish doesn't know that it's wet," and that's true, unless of course it finds itself flopping around on a dock. I think that's what we're like. Without intentional intervention, we're rarely aware of our assumptions. We assume that our air is just, well, air, unless our attention is drawn to it for some reason. Sometimes that intervention is pleasant, like traveling up into the mountains and breathing clean air and saying, "Oh! This is what air is supposed to be like!" At other times, though, it is an unpleasant experience, like having a paramedic slap an oxygen mask on your face because your lungs have finally had enough. Generally speaking, we're *all* oblivious to our environment and our assumptions, unless something or Someone breaks through our "normal" and turns everything on its head.

Opening the Eyes of the Unconsciously Blind

Jesus broke through to Mary and Cleopas on Easter Sunday as they were walking home. They were unconsciously breathing the religious air they had always breathed, without being aware of how blind they were to truth and why that blindness resulted in such pain. It took the devastation of Jesus' crucifixion to begin to arouse them to see their faulty assumptions.

In the same way that Jesus gave sight to physically blind people, he opened the disciples' blind eyes, too. Their blindness had led to despair, sadness, and confusion. They had breathed in religious assumptions about themselves, God, and their nation, and the thought that there might be a different perspective than the one they were accustomed to would be like discovering you were blind, when all your life you thought you could see. *Impossible!* they might have thought.

Like us, they held certain beliefs that were as second nature as breathing. First of all, they were shocked that their Messiah had been crucified. They believed that, as David's true Son, the Christ would reestablish a powerful monarchy in Israel. They thought he would overthrow the Romans. Instead of victory, they were dumbfounded by Rome's ongoing oppression. They were also confused by strange reports about the resurrection, even though they had heard them from trusted friends. The events of the past few days had been unthinkable simply because their religious assumptions were completely wrong.

A Painful Healing

Let's take another look now at the surprising words those travelers heard on the Emmaus road. Perhaps there we'll begin to see how, like them, we might have an interpretation of the Bible that clashes with its Author.

After asking them what they were talking about, Jesus' next words to them appear unkind at best, perhaps even rude. Even though he obviously loved them, his words to them do seem harsh. He called them "foolish" and "slow of heart." No matter what culture you're from, those aren't terms of endearment. We might have expected him to speak comfort to them—after all, they had just gone through the most traumatic event of their lives. But that's not how our loving Rabboni spoke to them. They had just been jolted into a new reality. He wasn't going to allow them to slide back into sleepy delusions. He said, "O foolish ones, and slow of heart to believe all that the prophets have spoken! Was it not necessary that the Christ should suffer these things and enter into his glory?" (Luke 24:25–26).

Why would Jesus speak to them in this way? Why call them "foolish" and "slow of heart"? What was he getting at? He certainly didn't want to make them feel worse than they already did.

Let's consider his words. The word *foolish* didn't mean that he thought they were silly or ignorant. They didn't have an IQ problem. They were "foolish" and "slow of heart" because they held an unconscious, blind allegiance to error. The truth is that they were actually *unwilling* to see the truth.[1] Though they loved Jesus, they refused to believe what he said when it contradicted their long-held expectations. Their misunderstanding (and subsequent sadness) was a faith problem, an unwillingness to embrace God's story instead of their own. They wanted to star in their own production of *It's a Wonderful Life*, so in the same way that they were unable to recognize the stranger who was talking to them, they refused to hear what Jesus had spoken before his death. His words *I'm going up to Jerusalem to die but I will rise after three days* (see Mark 10:33–34) found no foothold in their hearts. They weren't able to rest in the goodness of his plan or in his power to see it through because they wouldn't hear of it. In the same way that Peter rebuked Jesus for predicting his death, they refused to believe that God's loving plan might mean suffering *before* glory or that it would be something other than great worldly success. So even though Jesus had warned them over and over again about what was about to happen, when his death did come, their world fell apart. They refused to allow for any possibility that life would not turn out as they had planned. They likely pictured themselves on thrones, expelling the Romans, and ruling over the Gentiles rather than welcoming them into God's family.

Was Jesus being unkind in speaking to them in this way? No, of course not! Because of his deep love for them, he refused to allow them to stay in spiritual darkness. He spoke to them only the truth and only in love. He wanted to free them from their misery. But because they had been willfully blind, he had to pry open their eyes, partly through the gut-wrenching suffering they had just gone through, but also through the work of the Spirit as he spoke to them.

This Is Not the Story I Signed Up For

We aren't so different from them, are we? I know I'm not. I, too, want to read assurances of daily deliverance and guarantees of worldly success in the Bible, even though that's not its message. When we try to make the Bible all about us, when we miss the overarching story of the Redeemer's suffering and glory, its message gets twisted all out of shape. Sometimes we hope it will guarantee that we will be able to control our lives, that our future will be bright, or that we'll understand the "why" of everything that happens to us. But then, when things don't turn out the way we think God has promised, we become dejected, confused, and hopeless, like our friends on the Emmaus road. And the Bible seems insipid and worthless. Rather, it is only when we learn the lesson that Jesus taught that we will be able to persevere in the difficulties we inevitably face. Only then will the Bible blaze to life before our eyes. "As he talked, their hearts, previously chilled by disappointment and confusion, got warmer and warmer, to the ignition point."[2] They began to see what we'll eventually see:

our Savior in his leading role, as the one who loved us and who is the point of everything that was ever written in the Scriptures from beginning to end.

Once the three travelers reached their destination, they shared bread with him and finally realized his true identity. Upon this discovery, Cleopas and Mary were no longer sad or dejected. They were no longer foolish or slow of heart. They were energized. Their eyes had been opened. Immediately they returned to Jerusalem and joined with the rest of the disciples, sharing the good news (Luke 24:30–34). *Jesus is alive! The Scriptures have been fulfilled!* They were no longer sad, retreating, or confused. They were filled with joyful wonder. But they were in for even more surprises.

Suddenly the Lord appeared in their midst. After assuring them that it really was him, he said,

> "These are my words that I spoke to you while I was still with you, that everything written about me in the Law of Moses and the Prophets and the Psalms must be fulfilled." Then he opened their minds to understand the Scriptures.
>
> Luke 24:44–45

This is Jesus' second class on that Sunday. This time he taught all his disciples, not just Mary and Cleopas, how to read the Scriptures. Did you notice that on this occasion, though, he says that not only Moses and the Prophets but also the Psalms spoke of him? Luke wants us to see that Jesus reinterpreted the entire body of sacred writings, from Genesis to Malachi, as being about him.

Once again, Jesus "opened their minds" (Luke 24:45). They, too, had been foolish and slow of heart, but he enabled them to see the events of the last few days as part of one cohesive message of suffering and glory. What was the essence of that one message? *Nothing less than the gospel!*

> [Jesus] said to them, "Thus it is written, that the Christ should suffer and on the third day rise from the dead, and that repentance *for the forgiveness of sins* should be proclaimed in his name to all nations, beginning from Jerusalem."
>
> Luke 24:46–47

Jesus said that the overarching message of the entire Bible is that God is lovingly calling his children, beloved daughters and sons, back to himself through his life, death, and resurrection, and bestowing on people from all nations the indescribable gift of the forgiveness of sins. All people can be forgiven. Women and men.

Everything recorded in the Scriptures, all the way from Genesis through Revelation, is the proclamation of this gospel message. It is the message of the woman's Son who would crush the head of her children's Enemy (see Genesis 3:15). It is the story of a terribly broken world in desperate need of a Redeemer, where those who seemed to be heroic, like Noah, soon find themselves in drunkenness and depravity. It is the message of a weak-willed, childless idolater being chosen to bring blessing to the entire world. It's the story of his surprising faith and the cry of the Lord to spare Abraham's son on Mount Moriah because the sacrificial Son had already been chosen. And it's the story of God's nation, Israel, and their futile search for a good King who would rule righteously and truly deliver them from all their enemies. He would join them to all the other nations of the earth. Every genealogy, every law, song, prophecy, and promise is inextricably bound to this one story: *God is calling*

daughters and sons of every nationality to return to him and find
welcome and the forgiveness of sins.

We'll begin to read the Bible the way Jesus taught when we
recognize that the gospel message wasn't first preached by John
the Baptist when he declared Jesus "the Lamb of God" who would
take away the sins of the world" (John 1:29). Rather, it had been
declared over and over again for thousands of years, sometimes in
messages as bright as the noonday sun, and other times in shadows
and weakness. But the story of the Son's suffering, his glorification,
and our salvation will be as plain as day when the Spirit opens our
eyes and makes our hearts willing to receive his message.

Empowered by Jesus' Word and Spirit

Over the next forty days, until his ascension, Jesus spent intensive
hours teaching his followers how to interpret the Old Testament.
He taught them what his kingdom looked like and the real trajec-
tory of his plan: a plan built around the message of good news
for the entire world. The time he spent teaching them resulted in
the New Testament being written as it was, rooted firmly in the
Old Testament, which is why it is filled with so many allusions,
references, and even direct quotations from the Old. That the
disciples took Jesus' message to heart is proven by the fact that
there are 343 exact quotations from the Old Testament in the New
(not counting the hundreds of allusions).[3] They were listening!

As you'll soon discover, the gospel isn't a subplot or after-
thought in the Old Testament. It is the whole message, which is
why the earliest missionaries, like Peter and Paul, used it to prove
that Jesus was the Christ.

I've heard many sermons over the years about how the fearful
disciples were transformed into fearless apostles by the outpour-

ing of the Spirit at Pentecost. They were "clothed with power" (Luke 24:48–49) and became bold witnesses of the things they had seen and heard. And while that is certainly true, the bestowal of the Holy Spirit wasn't the only event that transformed them after the resurrection. Their understanding of the Scriptures was radically reconfigured. The blinders were removed. They became convinced by the risen Christ that God's plan would inevitably succeed and that the Jesus they had come to know and love was, in fact, the Messiah who would bring blessing to all the nations of the earth. They had finally learned how to read and interpret the Scriptures.

Peter's Transformation

The difference between Peter the disciple who cowered in shame before a servant girl's accusations and the confident apostle who preached a sermon to thousands, was the result of *both* the empowering of the Holy Spirit and a Christ-centered understanding of the Scriptures. The change in Peter speaks not only of his infilling by the Spirit at Pentecost but also to his spending forty days in Jesus' school of Bible interpretation. How do we know? Listen carefully to the way Peter connected Jesus' resurrection to one of the psalms. Speaking of David, Peter quotes Psalm 16:10 and surprisingly applies it to Jesus: "[David] being therefore a prophet . . . foresaw and spoke about the resurrection of the Christ" (Acts 2:30–31). Did you catch that? Peter said David spoke about Jesus' resurrection!

Yes, Peter declared that David wrote about Jesus. Later, in his first letter to Christian exiles, Peter wrote that the Old Testament prophets spoke of the grace to come and wondered who it was that the "Spirit of Christ" in them was "indicating when he predicted the sufferings of Christ and the subsequent glories" (1 Peter 1:10–11). Can you hear the echo of Jesus' first sermon on suffering before glory?

The apostle Peter believed that the Old Testament prophets' words were not given to them generically by the Holy Spirit but rather by the very Spirit of Christ in and through them. In other words, Peter wanted to emphasize the Son's particular presence in the words of the prophets. It was the Son himself who was speaking through them about his person and work to come. The prophets didn't know about whom they were speaking. But when Jesus, the Son, read their writings, he knew they were talking about him. And now so did Peter.

Philip Interprets the Old Testament

Not only did Jesus spend time teaching principles of interpretation to the apostles who were to write much of the New Testament, he also taught Philip (a deacon in the Jerusalem church) how to read them. We know that Philip learned the true meaning of the Old Testament because he was sent to an Ethiopian eunuch returning from celebrating the Passover who couldn't understand the meaning of Isaiah 53. Philip joined him while he traveled from Jerusalem and taught him that the Suffering Servant of whom Isaiah spoke was Jesus (see Acts 8:26–29). Philip knew how to interpret the Old Testament in light of the gospel, and now so did this Ethiopian official, who would eventually bring the good news to Africa.

Paul's Radical Transformation

Paul, whose misunderstanding of the Old Testament had caused the imprisonment and slaughter of Christians, met the ascended Lord Jesus on a dusty road, too. After this meeting, he eventually became the foremost spokesman for the gospel. Just as in the Emmaus road experience, the Lord's message to Paul wasn't delivered on the wings of a dove or a pretty Instagram post. No, it was pretty much a slap-down from heaven. Jesus knocked Paul off his horse onto his knees and temporarily blinded him (Acts 9:1–8). Then Paul had to be led by hand into Damascus, where he fasted and heard the message of the gospel as he "received it through a revelation of Jesus Christ" (Galatians 1:12). It was there that he began to learn to interpret the Scriptures. The book of Acts records numerous sermons Paul gave connecting the Old Testament to Jesus. Here is how he defended himself before King Agrippa:

> "I stand here testifying . . . saying nothing but what the prophets and Moses said would come to pass: that the Christ must suffer and that, by being the first to rise from the dead, he would proclaim light both to our people and to the Gentiles."
>
> Acts 26:22–23

Do you think Paul would have been able to connect Moses' words with the life and death of the man from Nazareth without his own Emmaus-Damascus road experience? How could a fierce, Christ-hating zealot (think ISIS) write that Jesus was the One through whom the hidden plan of God would be made known to the Gentiles, of all people? (See Ephesians 3:8–9.) Could it be that Paul became the primary writer of gospel truth because he had already memorized so much of the Old Testament? When he finally came to see how Jesus of Nazareth fulfilled the Scriptures, his heart was set on fire and he set the entire ancient Near East ablaze, too.

Have You Been to Jesus' Sunday School?

Like the disciples, we, too, will be transformed from confusion and disillusionment to radiance when we see God's story woven throughout the whole Bible.

The Gospels (the first four books of the New Testament) aren't the only place the story of God the Son is communicated. In fact, there's hardly a place in the Scriptures that doesn't testify to him. Sadly, very few people understand this. And when we fail to understand, Scripture reading loses its attraction. It's not unusual for women who love God's Word to be mistaken about how it should be interpreted, and, because of that, find it boring or confusing. Here are some typical ways we may fail to read his Word rightly.

The Magic 8 Ball Method

Some women read the Bible hoping to discover a particular message that will enable them to discern God's will for their lives in a specific circumstance. They might want to know if they should move to Atlanta, change churches, marry a certain person, or wear blue or brown shoes. I call this the Magic 8 Ball method of reading. It's what we do when we want direct revelation from the Lord. Of course, the problem is that the Bible was never meant to function in this way, and just like the Magic 8 Ball, this way of interacting with Scripture has more to do with "magic" or chance than Jesus and his gospel. When we use the Bible in this way, we end up disappointed and disillusioned. The Bible was not written to give us specific answers to daily questions. It does provide general guidelines about life, but its primary message is about salvation by faith, Jesus, and the gospel. The Bible was *never* meant to be used like a Magic 8 Ball . . . or as my Magic 8

Ball used to answer my questions when I was a child, "Not at this time." Or ever.

The Headlines Method

When I first became a Christian, in the early 1970s, there were numerous bestsellers about how something happening in a certain part of the world was a fulfillment of end-time prophecies. And even today, in certain segments of Christianity, it's a common practice to hold the Bible in one hand and news headlines in the other. I can understand why this way of reading Scripture is enticing: It seems to make the Bible relevant and exciting. It bolsters the faith of those who aren't quite sure the Bible is true, so they can say, "See? The Bible really is right!" when a current event seems to confirm what a prophet predicted. It also helps to make sense of what appears to be a world spinning out of control. It might seem exciting to predict coming events, but when that third blood moon doesn't bring about the events you were expecting, it can get pretty discouraging. While it is true that many Christians do view certain events in the Middle East as direct fulfillment of Scripture, it's probably best to take a very loose view of them and not try to use them as proof that the Bible is correct. Newspaper headlines don't prove the truth of the Bible. The resurrection does.

The Quid Pro Quo Method

Other women read the Bible because they believe it is their duty and expect that God will bless their day when they start it out with his Word. Let's call this the Quid Pro Quo Method. Quid pro quo means "this for that" or "a favor for a favor." I once spoke with a dear sister who thought the reason she had a flat tire on her way to work was because she had failed to read the Bible that morning. Once again, when you read the Bible as a guarantee that good will come to you or as a talisman against adversity, you'll soon be cynical and apathetic. God isn't a genie in a bottle who will grant us three wishes if we spend devotional time with him before our day begins. Bible reading is meant to clothe you in faith so that when either blessing or adversity (or the boringly mundane) confront you, you'll be enabled to face them with courage and humility, remembering the story of how you've been loved throughout the ages. We don't read the Bible to earn God's blessing. We read it because his blessing is already ours.

The WWHD Method

Other women read because they believe the Bible is made up of good moral lessons. They haven't yet made the connection between the story of Abraham's offering up of Isaac and the heavenly Father's offering of his Son, so they read Abraham's story and think the reason it is there is to encourage them to offer up all their "Isaacs." They read stories about Jesus feeding the five thousand and interpret it to mean they should be willing to give up lunch. To them, the story of Peter walking on the water means that they should try extraordinary things for God. I call this the What Would Heroes Do? Method (WWHD). They look at these stories and immediately think: *That story must be there to tell me what I should do.* And while it's not wrong to seek to live lives of faith and obedience, it is not the primary reason those stories appear in Scripture. They are there to point us to Jesus, the only truly faithful hero. When you read with the WWHD Method, you'll end up in either despair or pride. You'll be despairing when you try to act like Peter and sink under the waves, or you'll be proud like Peter when you think you've got it all together—Jesus must be crazy when he talks about his death and your denial. The stories aren't there to tell us how to become heroes. They are there to reveal the One True Hero.

There are two problems with these four Bible-reading methods: The first is that you may ignore the original intent of the writer. As much as we can, we want to try to discern how the original readers would have interpreted a particular passage. In other words, what did David mean when he said "The Lord is my shepherd"? The second problem with these methods is that the gospel becomes secondary. The life, death, resurrection, and ascension of Jesus is assumed and glossed over. *"Sure, the gospel is important . . . but only as a first step,"* they say. Or *"The real action is in discerning a specific word from God or a specific command or meaning of future events. The Bible is magical; it protects against any harm and guarantees a blessing."*

Class Registration Is Open

My dear sisters, no matter how you've been reading your Bible, or even if you haven't been reading it at all, I've got great news for you. You're about to step into Jesus' classroom. You are going to become a Bible interpreter. The only prerequisite for entry is a desire to learn. Rabboni Jesus will be happy to welcome you, and you'll be happy you signed up. As we begin now to go to the Scriptures, don't be surprised if your heart begins to warm up to the prospect of reading as you begin to see him everywhere . . . though, of course, like those early learners, you might feel a pinch when the blinders are removed. I know you want to become a woman who knows how to "rightly" handle the word of truth (2 Timothy 2:15). You'll do that when you start to read both the Old Testament and the New with this thought in mind: "Remember Jesus Christ, risen from the dead, the offspring of David" (2 Timothy 2:8).

Open Bible, Open Heart

1. What do you think the Lord might want to gently speak to you today? Do you think he might say that, like the disciples he dearly loved, you, too, are foolish or slow to believe? It's not cruel or harsh to ask those kinds of questions, because our Rabboni, the one who loves us and loves to enable us to understand truth, wants to free us from any sadness and confusion that our misreading of the Bible may produce. Do you want to have your mind and heart opened? What might that be like?

2. Peter, Philip, and Paul each attended Jesus' school of Bible interpretation. How do you feel about signing up for the same course they took?

3. I listed several common methods of reading the Bible. Do you see yourself in any of those descriptions? Which one(s)? Are you convinced that those ways are not the ways Jesus would teach you to read? Why or why not?

---

4. Summarize what you've learned in this chapter in four or five sentences.

For Further Study

1. Read a few of the sermons that Peter and Paul preached in the book of Acts (see 3:12–26; 4:8–12; 10:34–43; 13:16–41; 17:22–31; 26:1–23), trying to discern how they used the Old Testament. Where do you hear them reiterating the message of suffering before glory?

---

2. How would learning to read the Bible in this Christocentric manner change your perspective on Bible reading? Can you

pinpoint a passage or two that might be changed by reading it as solely being about Jesus?

_____

_____

_____

_____

_____

3

Finding the Love of Jesus in the Books of Moses

"For if you believed Moses, you would believe me; for he wrote of me."

John 5:46

It is commonly accepted that Moses, the man who led Israel out of Egypt, authored the first five books of the Bible, Genesis through Deuteronomy.[1] In them, Moses tells the story of the creation of the world as well as the creation of the nation of Israel. He records the law given by God on Mount Sinai and chronicles Israel's wandering through the wilderness after their deliverance from Egypt. This section is sometimes called "The Books of the Law," though it is much more than a big list of dos and don'ts. While there are laws, much of it records the history of God's people, starting with Adam, and the forming of the nation of Israel all the way through to their entrance into the promised land. This section should be read as both God's Law and Israel's history. But that's not all. Moses also preaches the gospel and tells us about Jesus.

"Wait a minute, Elyse!" you might be thinking, *"I've read those first five books and I've never seen anything about Jesus or the gospel there!"* I understand your objection. And if it hadn't been Jesus himself who made the claim that Moses had written about him, I would be shouting "Foul!" right along with you.

Those Are Fighting Words

Before we search the Pentateuch for actual examples of the gospel, let's look at the context for Jesus' claim that Moses actually wrote about him. On one occasion, when the religious leaders were harassing Jesus because he had healed on the Sabbath, he confronted them about their blindness. He told them that because they refused to hear his word, they didn't have eternal life. He said that though they claimed to believe in Moses and his writings, they had failed to see what was right before their eyes.

> You search the Scriptures because you think that in them you have eternal life; and it is they that bear witness about me. . . . For if you believed Moses, you would believe me; for he wrote of me. But if you do not believe his writings, how will you believe my words?
>
> John 5:39, 46–47

Jesus said belief in his words would bring eternal life, and he told the religious leaders that they would die because they failed to grasp the truth about who he was. Like our Emmaus road friends, their inability to see wasn't the result of simple ignorance. It was a moral failing. They refused to believe that a Messiah would be born under such questionable circumstances, that he would befriend women, sinners, the sick, the Gentiles, and that he wouldn't flatter them or prop up their positions. Instead of shunning the Romans, he healed their servants. He touched people who were "unclean" and received the worship of children and immoral women. Every class of person that the religious leaders despised, Jesus loved. They refused to see that as Israel's Son he didn't come to crush the "unworthy" but rather to save them.

Think again about what Jesus said to them: Moses declared that Jesus was the Christ. Belief in this truth about Jesus written by Moses would eventuate in their salvation, while unbelief would damn them. How important is it to see that Moses wrote about Jesus? For them, it meant their eternal souls. They viewed Moses as a religious leader, a hero to be emulated. Jesus said he was primarily a witness to him.

The apostle Paul understood the truth about the gospel in the Pentateuch. In fact, Paul based his entire message of salvation by faith alone on Genesis 15:6. In that verse, Moses says Abraham was "counted righteous" because he believed in God's promise of a Son. In other words, Paul believed that the very words of Moses about Abraham's faith-righteousness were actually written to encourage and strengthen us! They tell us how salvation comes to us!

Did Moses understand the full implication of what he was writing when he recorded that story about Abraham? Probably not, but,

One can imagine Moses saying, "Well, I never thought of it that way, but now that you come to say it like that, I can see where you got it, and I like it"; that is, he would not think that his original intent had been violated.[2]

I trust that you're beginning to see how reading the Old Testament in a gospel-centered way isn't just a gimmick. Rather, it's your very life.

Here He Is . . . and Here . . . and Here . . .

There are several ways to see Jesus and the gospel in the writings of Moses (and in the entire Old Testament). Throughout the remainder of this study, as we proceed through all the different parts of the Old Testament, I'm going to point some out so that you can learn to employ them yourselves. Of course, in this short book, I won't be able to identify every instance of each of them, but you'll soon be able to discover them for yourself. The various keys to finding Jesus and the gospel in the Old Testament can be discovered by considering any of these four categories:

Physical appearances of the Son *before* Bethlehem

- Did the Son make any appearances in this section before he actually appeared as a baby in Bethlehem?
- How can we identify those appearances and what might they tell us about the gospel message?
- Did the writers of the New Testament see him there, too?

Prophetic words about the Son

- Does anyone in this section speak about people or events in a way that points us forward to the gospel?
- Did the writers of the New Testament confirm this by quoting or alluding to those prophecies?

Types of the Son in his person and work

- In this section, do we see anyone mediating between God and man or offering himself or an acceptable sacrifice to impede anticipated judgment?

Gospel story: How does this passage foretell the gospel message? How does it declare the need for a Savior?

- Is the gospel story being foreshadowed in any way?
  - ~ For instance, do we see someone who needs redeeming or someone who offers redemption?
  - ~ Do we see the motifs of the gospel: creation/fall/ redemption or obedience/judgment/grace or death/ burial/resurrection in any of the stories?

The Gospel in the Creation Story

In the story that Moses recorded about the creation and fall of Adam and Eve, we can easily see every one of these keys.

Physical Appearances of the Son before Bethlehem

Can we see the Son in the first week of creation? Sure. We hear him saying, "Let *us* make man in our image" (Genesis 1:26). Exactly who is the being referred to there by "us"? Most Christians believe it is a reference to the Trinity. In this instance, we don't actually see the Son, though he is the one who is speaking. We know this because Paul tells us that he is the one who created everything, including you and me (Colossians 1:16; 1 Corinthians 8:6).

Later, we learn of his physical entrance into the world (Genesis 3:8). The Son entered the garden of Eden every evening to walk with his children. Who was it who actually walked with them? Jesus, of course.[3] We know that it was the Son who walked with them because he is always the One who makes the invisible God known (John 1:18).

Here at the very beginning of human history, Jesus enjoyed sweet fellowship with Eve and Adam as they walked together through the garden. They expected him to come to them and talk at the end of the day. What bliss.

Prophetic Words

After their devastating fall into sin, Jesus passed judgment on them (John 5:22). The man will find work difficult because the creation itself will militate against him. The woman will suffer in her relationship with her husband and children, and will know pain in her labor to bring forth children. But in the midst of the heartache to come, the Son would come back into his world, this time to heal everything that had been shattered. Born of a woman, Jesus the promised one proclaimed that he would bruise the head of their Enemy, though he would suffer in doing so (Genesis 3:15). Woman, who was the cause of the suffering, will also be the conduit through whom relief from suffering and death would come. He loved her enough to give her a hope for the future.

Types of the Son

After Jesus pronounced words of both judgment and hope, he killed a beloved creature, which was the first death the world had ever known. Blood was spilled, and the Lord skinned his beautiful animal (was it a lamb?) in order to clothe his naked and shamed children. Do you see how the death of this animal and the subsequent clothing of the man and woman are a perfect type of Jesus and his loving work on our behalf? Jesus gave his life so that our nakedness and shame before God would be covered with his righteousness (Isaiah 61:10).

Adam and Eve were then driven out of the garden so that they wouldn't suffer the terrible judgment of eating from the Tree of Life and living forever as sinners. Yes, death entered into the world on that day, but our Savior didn't leave us alone. He promised that he would come to us and bring us back into his garden so that we would once again enjoy fellowship with him.

The Gospel Story

In these first pages of the Old Testament, we have the entire gospel story. It's frequently called the *proto-evangelion*, which means "the first gospel." Here we see the gospel message: that the Lord is determined to have a people with whom he can walk in fellowship in the cool of the day, and he will do everything necessary, including suffer, to make that happen.

Finding Jesus' Love in the Wilderness with Hagar

Let's fast-forward now to the story of Abraham and his wife, Sarah. God called Abraham and promised him a land and a son through whom he would bless the whole earth (Genesis 12:1–3). Although God had promised Abraham and Sarah a son, it had been ten years and still they were childless. So Sarah took matters into her own hands and gave her Egyptian slave, Hagar, to her husband so that he might father a child through her. Once Hagar conceived, she felt the wrath of Sarah and ran away (Genesis 16:6).

Jesus before Bethlehem

Now, listen to the story of Jesus' love for women, especially women who are powerless, in trouble, and even in rebellion: The "angel of the Lord" appeared to Hagar while she was in the wilderness. One of the ways to find Jesus before his appearance in Bethlehem is to look for instances like this one where *the angel of the Lord* appears or speaks.[4] Not every occurrence of someone called "the angel of the Lord" should be assumed to be the preincarnate Christ, but many can be. We can usually assume that a particular angel is the Son when he is called "the angel of the Lord"[5] and when he is referred to as "the Lord" at a different place in the passage, when he performs miracles, or when he doesn't refuse to receive worship. Remember that the word *angel* actually means "messenger," and Jesus certainly was that.[6] Jesus asked Hagar what she was doing wandering around in the wilderness before he sent her back to submit to Sarah. He promised her a son who would become a great nation and care for her.

Prophetic Words

In the entire recorded history of the world to that time, Hagar, a powerless Egyptian slave woman, is the first person to describe God's nature by naming him. Don't miss the importance of this. Although the Lord had revealed himself previously to others (Adam and Eve, Enoch, Noah, and Abraham and Sarah), none of them had been granted a revelation like this, one that spoke of a personal, intimate relationship. Later on, Abraham will call him *Jehovah Jireh* (the God who provides), but lowly Hagar is the first to be given this honor. What did she name him? *Lahai-roi*, which means "the Living One, who sees me."[7] Hagar said, "Truly here

I have seen him who looks after me" (Genesis 16:13). Isn't that a beautiful picture of the character of our Lord, the One who loves the powerless, the poor, the unwed and pregnant? He is the One who sees us as we are, knows all our needs, and cares for us (1 Peter 5:7). Hagar had no guarantee that the child she carried would be looked after by Abraham (though he was the father), and she was certain that Sarah wouldn't care for either of them. But now she knew that there was a God, a Living One, who would look after her and care for her. Later on, another powerless woman would learn the same lesson: Mary Magdalene learned that Jesus is her Living One who would see and care for her, too.

Type and Gospel Story

This story of Sarah, Hagar, and "the God who sees and cares for us," is a perfect picture of the gospel. Sarah had been chosen to be the one through whom the Messiah would eventually come, but she sinfully took matters into her own hands. Did her unbelief have consequences? Yes, of course, but these consequences couldn't derail God's plan to bless the entire world through her. Hagar is the perfect type of many women: friendless, powerless, and used, yet not overlooked by the Lord. This story speaks to every woman who finds herself in a terrible circumstance: Jesus is the one who sees us and "looks after us." He loves to care for and speak words of comfort to women, and so on this first appearance of "the angel of the Lord" (after the fall), he comes to an unmarried, pregnant, runaway slave girl. Jesus' heart is open to and aware of the suffering of his daughters. He sees and cares for us and he wants everyone to know it.

Do you see how this story is meant primarily to speak to us about the love and care of the Son and not primarily about something we should or should not do, or even about conflicts in the Middle East?

Finding Jesus' Love on Mount Moriah

After nearly two decades, Abraham's wife, Sarah, finally gave birth to Isaac. He was the promised child who would become a great nation and bring God's blessing to all the peoples of the earth; but before that could happen, God made a very strange request of Abraham: He asked him to sacrifice his only son, Isaac.

Jesus before Bethlehem

Up Mount Moriah Abraham and his son Isaac trudged. They carried the fire, the wood, and the knife. But just as Abraham was about to plunge the knife into the promised son, the angel of the Lord called to him, "Abraham, Abraham! . . . Do not lay your hand upon the boy." Abraham then saw a ram, caught in a thicket by its horns (Genesis 22:11–13). Who was the angel of the Lord who prevented Isaac's death? Again, we can assume that the angel of the Lord who stopped Abraham from killing Isaac, who provided a ram for the sacrifice, and who subsequently spoke blessing over Abraham's life and children, was the Son. Jesus would provide the sacrifice by taking on a mortal body, and would bless all of Abraham's children, including you and me, the children of faith (Galatians 3:7).

Prophecy

Abraham named that place *Jehovah Jireh*, or "the Lord will provide." Remember that Hagar said that he was the Living One, who sees and cares. Now Abraham proclaims, "On the mount of the Lord it shall be provided" (Genesis 22:14). Think of that. Mount Moriah is the future site of Jerusalem, the very place where Jesus, the promised Son, would die at his Father's will. God would provide the Lamb. This isn't a coincidence. The Lord sees, cares, and provides all that is necessary for our salvation. Sisters, the Lord doesn't expect you to provide the needed sacrifice for sin. He provides all you need.

Types and the Gospel Story

I don't think it's necessary to belabor our point here. Abraham's willingness to sacrifice his only son on Mount Moriah is more than adequate for us to make the connection we need from the writings of Moses straight to Jesus. Can you see how important it is not to turn this story into a moral lesson about how we should be like Abraham and be willing to give up the things we love most? This story isn't about us at all—though it's not wrong to desire to love him above all else. The story is here to give us a foreshadowing of how Jesus would give up his life to provide for us and to show his love of God the Father above all else. It's the story of the kind of love that lays down its life not only for its friends but also for its enemies.

Are you beginning to get excited as you see that the stories in the Old Testament are not meant primarily to tell you to get to work, but rather are gospel proclamations about the work that has already been done?

Finding Jesus' Love Leading His People in the Exodus

Most of us have read the story of Moses leading the children of Israel out of their slavery in Egypt. Second only to the actual gospel itself, the exodus is the primary story of God's loving deliverance of his people.

Jesus before Bethlehem

Moses' first encounter with the angel of the Lord was in the burning bush, where he "appeared to him in a flame of fire," and is called both "the Lord" and "God" (Exodus 3:2–4). Who was calling Moses into ministry and with whom was he arguing later in this passage? The Son. Did Moses write about Jesus? Yes, of course he did. In fact, he carried on a conversation with him. The Son had heard his people's cry for rescue so he came down to them and sent them a deliverer. Whom did the Lord choose to deliver his people? An aged escaped murderer who had been hiding out in the wilderness for forty years (yes, that was Moses). The Lord loves to call and equip people who have no hope of rescue or usefulness.

Paul picks up this appearance of the preincarnate Christ and makes some shocking statements in 1 Corinthians 10. Not only did the Lord (Jesus) appear to Moses at his call, he also accompanied him throughout his wilderness wandering. Where do we see him? We see him in the cloud that led and the fire that warmed and protected the nation (Psalm 78:14). We see him quenching their thirst from the "Rock that followed them." Do you know who that Rock was? Paul is stunningly specific when he writes, "the Rock was Christ" (1 Corinthians 10:4). Here we see Paul interpreting "the Old Testament in a way that is centered on Christ . . . the leader of a new exodus."[8] (See also Exodus 23:20–23.)

But Paul isn't the only one who said Jesus accompanied them in the wilderness wandering. Jesus himself said he was the manna they ate: "My Father gives you the true bread from heaven. For the bread of God is he who comes down from heaven and gives life to the world. . . . I am the bread of life" (John 6:32–33, 35).

On several occasions Jesus identified himself as bread given to nourish his people. It's no wonder then that Mary and Cleopas finally recognized the stranger who spoke to them "in the breaking of the bread" (Luke 24:35). Jesus has been known for thousands of years in the breaking of bread at the Communion meal. He is the Cloud, the Fire, the Rock, the Bread. He is everywhere.

Prophecy

Moses prophesied of the coming of Jesus when he said, "The Lord your God will raise up for you a prophet like me from among you, from among your brothers—it is to him you shall listen" (Deuteronomy 18:15).

Jesus wasn't being narcissistic when he claimed that Moses wrote of him. He had read this prophecy like any other young Jewish boy. But there was one difference: None of them identified themselves like Jesus did as being "the Prophet" that Moses spoke about. The Jews were looking for a prophet to come, which was why they asked John the Baptist if he was the Christ, Elijah, or "the Prophet" (John 1:20–21). John said he wasn't the Prophet, but only the voice of one crying in the wilderness.

Jesus claimed that he would finally be recognized as the Prophet at his crucifixion: "Then you will know that I am he, and that I do nothing on my own authority, but speak just as the Father taught me" (John 8:28). He was the one the people would listen to: "For I have not spoken on my own authority, but the Father who sent me has himself given me a commandment—what to say and what to speak. . . . What I say, therefore, I say as the Father has told me" (John 12:49–50).

Can you see how Jesus is the perfect fulfillment of the words Moses spoke? He was an Israelite, from the house of David. He was from "among their brothers." He also acknowledged that the words he spoke were not his own idea but that he was obediently conveying what the Father said to him. He was like us, human, and yet not like us, in that he faithfully delivered words that were in accord with his Father's will. His words have the power to bring eternal life. The Lord promised to redeem his people and take them for himself: "I will take you to be my people, and I will be your God" (Exodus 6:7). Over and over again through the entire exodus story, Moses prophesied about the deliverance the Lord would bring about for his people.

Type

The number of types of Christ that fill the story of the Exodus are almost too numerous to mention, but here's a familiar one: The night before the tenth plague fell on the Egyptians, a perfect lamb, one without blemish, had to be slaughtered. The blood of this sacrifice had to be placed on the doorposts of their houses so that the death angel would *pass over* them. The apostle Peter believed Jesus' interpretation of the Old Testament sacrifices when he wrote that we were ransomed from our former way of life by "the precious blood of Christ, like that of a lamb without blemish or spot" (1 Peter 1:19; see also Hebrews 9:14).[9]

Gospel Message

Moses told the story of the good news of the love of a Savior who is willing to be sacrificed to bring his children out of bondage and slavery. The most important message in the exodus story is that the Lord sees and knows us and has taken measures to free us, forgive us, and make us his own, all through the slaughter of one final perfect Lamb, his Son. Do you see how Moses' telling of the exodus story isn't primarily about our duty to be more like Moses? The first thing we should see when we read Exodus is that, like the Israelites, we've been made recipients of God's gracious love and sacrifice.

Warming Heart

I hope that now you're beginning to understand how seeing Jesus in the books of Moses, indeed in all the Old Testament, will change the way you read it. Perhaps now, when you read the narratives of creation, the exodus, or the wilderness wanderings, you can do so without first asking, "What do these verses tell me to do?" or "How can I be like this person or avoid being like that one?" Instead, I trust that you'll read these events as though they were good news to you about the Living One who sees, provides, and cares for even the lowliest among us.

OPEN BIBLE, OPEN HEART

1. Jesus said Moses wrote about him. What were your thoughts about that statement before you read this chapter? Are you more convinced now that he was right?

   _____

   _____

   _____

2. There are a number of passages that reference the "angel of the Lord" in the Pentateuch, the first five books of the Old Testament. What do you learn about his visitations from the following verses?

a. Genesis 16:7–11

b. Genesis 22:11–15

c. Exodus 3:2

d. Exodus 14:19

e. Numbers 22:22–35

3. Much of the Pentateuch concerns ceremonial sacrifices and laws. How might these things speak to us about the gospel message?

4. In his letter to the Romans, Paul said that what Moses wrote was "not written for his sake alone, but for ours also . . . who believe in him who raised from the dead Jesus our Lord"

(Romans 4:22–24). How do Moses' words encourage us to believe the gospel message?

_____

_____

_____

5. Summarize what you've learned in this chapter in four or five sentences.

_____

_____

_____

_____

FOR FURTHER STUDY

1. Pick one story you're familiar with in the Pentateuch and see if you can find connections in it to Jesus. Write out your findings.

_____

_____

_____

2. "For I tell you that Christ became a servant to the circumcised to show God's truthfulness, in order to confirm the promises given to the patriarchs, and in order that the Gentiles might glorify God for his mercy" (Romans 15:8–9). What promises "given to the patriarchs" were confirmed by the gospel story?

_____

_____

_____

_____

3. Paul wrote that "the Scripture, foreseeing that God would justify the Gentiles by faith, preached the gospel beforehand to Abraham, saying, 'In you shall all the nations be blessed'" (Galatians 3:8). In other words, Paul believed that Abraham had heard the gospel message and was saved because he believed it (see Galatians 3:6). What was the message Abraham heard? What was the result of his faith?

_____

_____

_____

_____

4

Finding the Love of Jesus in Israel's Stories

"Blessed be the Lord, who has not left you this day without a redeemer."

Ruth 4:14

The history of Israel recorded in the twelve books from Joshua through Esther spans about eight hundred years and makes up the second genre or type of literature found in the Old Testament. This section is usually referred to as "history" and records events that began with the nation's possession of the land of Canaan through to their loss of the land, and then their partial resettlement.[1] It tells the story of Joshua's conquests, the terrible brokenness when people do what is right in their own eyes, and the stories of women and men who were important in the preservation of the nation through whom the promised Son would come. They tell the story of Israel's unmet desire for a godly king,

71

their continual battles with enemies within, such as unbelief and idolatry, and enemies without, the nations that surrounded them.

These books also contain the story of how, though they anticipated the arrival of a Messiah, the people had forgotten their primary identity as a conduit of blessing to "all the families of the earth" (Genesis 12:3). They were to make the name of Yahweh known and revered by all people so that all people would be blessed. But instead of declaring how wonderful Yahweh was, they imitated the nations that surrounded them, embracing their gods. Proudly, they also thought of themselves as better than the nations around them. They looked down on them, and held themselves aloof from those whom they thought were not as pure as they were. These pages make it very clear that all people, even those chosen by God, need a Savior.

Since these books are full of stories about people of faith, it would be easy to think the stories are there so that we can aspire to become heroes, too. For instance, it might be easy to think that if we acted faithfully in the same way Ruth did, God would provide us with a rich husband like Boaz. But if we read these books like that, we are missing the point. They are here to help us prepare for and receive the long-awaited King, the only One who can deliver us from all our enemies. These histories do present a true record written about real people. But they are meant to illustrate God's work of redemption through his people, culminating with the birth of Jesus, the One who was worshiped by Gentile kings at his birth (Matthew 2:11). He was the promised One who would bring the worldwide blessing first promised to Eve and Adam.

As we consider this section of the Old Testament, we're going to look at stories in which women figure prominently so that you can see how the good news of Jesus' love is present in women's stories (not just in men's). Of course, David and Solomon figure largely in the history books, but we'll save our discussion of them for the next chapter.

Finding Jesus' Love Leading Deborah

Let's begin our study in Judges 4 with the story of our sister Deborah. We learn about her at a time when the people of Israel were being punished for their idolatry. Oppressed by the Canaanites, they cried out to the Lord for deliverance. In his mercy, the Lord answered their prayer by speaking to them through Deborah, a woman renowned for her wisdom. In her role as a prophetess, she delivered God's message to Barak, a military leader. She told him it was time to gather his army together because God would be with him as he fought his enemies (Judges 4:6–7). Although it wasn't customary for women to go into battle, Barak refused to go to war unless Deborah accompanied him, which she agreed to do—though she warned him that the glory for his upcoming victory would not fall to him but rather to a woman (Jael). God's rout of the Canaanites that day ended with the death of Sisera, a mighty leader who died on the floor of a woman's tent with a peg through his skull. Think of it, Sisera, a man "who had tormented Israel for twenty years, was destroyed by a homemaker."[2] Judges 5 records the song of victory that Deborah and Barak sang on that day. Now, if Jesus was right, we should be able to see his story, the gospel, in these events. So, where is he?

Jesus before Bethlehem

How should we think about the story of Deborah, Barak, Sisera, and his executioner, Jael? First, it is the true history of real people who fought an actual battle. That is its first and most obvious use. It tells us about something that actually happened. It is history.

But this story also functioned as a great national victory in David's mind, so he referenced it in one of his psalms. Then, hundreds of years later, Paul, the one who had been taught by Jesus how to read his nation's history, picked up on David's words and surprisingly applied them to Jesus' death and resurrection. What caused Paul to make these connections between Deborah, David, and Jesus? The Holy Spirit had opened his eyes to see the gospel in Israel's stories. So Paul declared that it was actually Jesus who routed Sisera's armies that day and that his victory prefigured Christ's ultimate victory over our enemies: death, sin, and Satan.[3]

Prophetic Words That Point Us to Christ

Deborah's prophecy that God would destroy Israel's enemies included this encouragement: "Does not the Lord go out before you?" I, too, am comforted to know that it is Jesus who goes out before us. He is the forerunner, the first One who walked through death and opened the door into life for us to follow. He is the "founder and perfecter of our faith" (Hebrews 12:2). He is the One who has promised to be with us, to never leave us or forsake us. Because he is here with us, we should never fear or be dismayed. (See Deuteronomy 31:8; Hebrews 13:5–6.) "Behold," he said, "I am with you always, to the end of the age" (Matthew 28:20). Jesus is the one who goes before us and fights victoriously over his enemies and ours.

Types of the Gospel Story

In this story, where do we see people whose actions remind us of Jesus, the King who conquers all our enemies? Like Jael, the comparatively weak housewife who crushed the head of her enemy while he lay sleeping on her floor, Jesus is the weak (in his human sense) crucified One, who crushed the skull of his Enemy even as his Roman adversaries were pounding spikes into his hands and feet. The gospel proves that God loves to bring our "rescue from a surprising source."[4] Jesus is the conquering King, who "disarmed the rulers and authorities and put them to open shame, by triumphing over them" (Colossians 2:15).

Even though the people of Israel had repeatedly done evil in God's sight and were suffering for it, God raised up valiant women to speak forth his Word, lead his people, and crush their Enemy's head. It would be very hard to read this story and not be reminded about the prophecy found in Genesis 3:15—that deliverance would come through a woman's offspring who would crush Satan's skull.

Is the point of this story that we should try to be like Deborah or Jael? No, it's that God uses the weak to accomplish deliverance, and that he will vanquish all his enemies through the seemingly weak message of the cross (1 Corinthians 1:27).

Finding Jesus' Faithful Love in Ruth's Story

Since there are only two books named after women, both in this section of the Old Testament, let's see how they speak about the gospel to us.

Ruth's story begins at a time of famine in Bethlehem. Elimelech, a Bethlehemite, his wife, Naomi, and their two sons journeyed from their home to Moab to try to find food. While there, the sons married Moabite women and subsequently all three men died. Naomi was left a childless widow. Then, while gleaning grain in the fields of Moab with her two daughters-in-law,

Naomi heard that the Lord had provided bread to his people in Bethlehem, so she decided to go home. Assuming that her life as a wife and mother was completely over, Naomi advised her daughters-in-law to stay in Moab and try to find husbands in their home country. One of the daughters took her advice, but Ruth refused to leave Naomi. So Naomi and Ruth both returned to Bethlehem, and Ruth went into the field of one of Naomi's relatives, Boaz, to gather what the reapers left behind. Boaz saw her, favored and protected her, and through a series of circumstances, became her kinsman-redeemer and married her. Then "the Lord gave her conception" (Ruth 4:13) and she bore a son, Obed, who was the grandfather of David, the king.

How should we read this story? Again, the first way is to read it as it is: the true history of real women and their ultimate rescue. It is about two destitute women living on the edge of starvation who were in need of gracious rescue. One had lost everything, but another, a despised foreigner, was about to be grafted into the genealogy of not only King David but also King Jesus.

Are you already seeing gospel clues in this story? Bethlehem, the need for bread, the rescue brought about by a redeemer, and a kingly line continued through women with no rights ought to remind you of Jesus and his story.

Jesus before Bethlehem

Where do we see Jesus in this story? Although we can't point out a visitation from "the angel of the Lord," we can recognize that it was the Lord who visited his people and gave them food (Ruth 1:6). It isn't unusual to see Jesus providing bread for the hungry . . . and even claiming to be the very bread God sent to his people (John 6). As in the story of Deborah, we don't see anyone who claims to be the angel of the Lord or who shows up to multiply bread, but we do see his activity in the background.

Prophetic Words Point to the Person and Work of Jesus

At the birth of Obed, Ruth's son, the women who surrounded Naomi exclaimed: "Blessed be the Lord who has not left you this day without a redeemer" (Ruth 4:14). To which we reply, "Amen!" Naomi had returned to her hometown, bent down in shame, proclaiming her new name *Bitter*. If we were writing this story without remembering the gospel, we might be tempted to say something like,

> Well, you know, Naomi, if you hadn't left Bethlehem and gone to live in Moab (which you know is against God's Law), and if you hadn't let your sons marry pagan women (which is also against God's Law), your life wouldn't be such a train wreck right now. So instead of feeling sorry for yourself, maybe you should just repent, learn to be thankful for what you have, and try to do what is right from now on.

Instead, this story tells us about a Redeemer who doesn't abandon broken women but rather sustains and cares for them. Can you tell how reading the Bible with the gospel in mind transforms this story from a morality tale into a sweet narrative of grace for the poor and the hopeless?

Type of Christ

The primary type of a Christ figure in this story is, of course, Boaz, the kinsman-redeemer who fulfills his familial responsibility to marry a foreigner and raise children for her and her mother-in-law's sake. And while he certainly is that, we can also see that Ruth is a type of Christ, too, as she makes a vow to stay with her bitter mother-in-law no matter what:

> "Where you go I will go, and where you lodge I will lodge. Your people shall be my people, and your God my God. Where you die I will die, and there will I be buried. May the Lord do so to me and more also if anything but death [and not even that] parts me from you."
>
> Ruth 1:16–17

Ruth became a living demonstration of the Lord's tender love and mercy. And just like Jesus, she was willing to be buried in a foreign land for the sake of the one she loved. Likewise, nothing, not even death, will part us from him:

> For I am sure that neither death nor life, nor angels nor rulers, nor things present nor things to come, nor powers, nor height nor depth, nor anything else in all creation, will be able to separate us from the love of God in Christ Jesus our Lord.
>
> Romans 8:38–39

Gospel Story

The gospel according to Ruth reminds us that before grace comes to us we are aliens and strangers, "having no hope and without God in the world" (Ephesians 2:12). Like Ruth and Naomi, we are desperate for a rescuer, a Redeemer, who will care for and rescue us. And like Ruth, we need the grace, or favor, of the Lord to rest upon us (Ruth 2:2, 13, 20), for without grace it will not matter how hard we work, it will never be enough. Our work will never be good enough or powerful enough to engraft us into the royal house of David. "Ultimately, for Christians, the grace of God is always the defining element of our lives."[5] Ruth's son,

Obed, became a restorer of life and nourished Naomi, no longer bitter, in her old age. What a beautiful portrait of the Lord's work through the gospel in our lives. We are restored and nourished even when all hope is gone.

Could we say that Elimelech's unwise move to Moab was sovereignly orchestrated by the Lord so that we might be assured that women without rights and who are destitute—even Moabite widows—can know that they are loved and welcomed by a gracious Savior? Of course, we must never assume that foolish decisions will eventuate in blessing or that disobedience is God's will, but we can say that God does use even the heartbreaking choices we make for his ultimate glory.

The Love of Jesus in the Life of Esther

This book opens with events occurring in the palace of King Ahasuerus, who ruled in Susa, a capital city in Persia. Through a series of nearly laughable occurrences, the king replaced his former queen with a young Jewess, Esther. At the same time, a high-ranking official, Haman, determined to exterminate all the Jewish exiles scattered throughout the Persian Empire. At the urging of her cousin Mordecai, Esther intervened on behalf of her people, and Haman's wicked scheme backfired, resulting in his being hanged on the gallows he had ordered built for Mordecai.

In approaching Esther's story, as I wrote in the notes for the book of Esther in the *ESV Gospel Transformation Bible*,

> It is typical to read Esther as a morality tale about cousins who stand in the gap to save a nation. As a consequence, women may be told, "Be faithful and wise like Esther!" But is Esther fundamentally a morality tale about how we should stand tall in the

midst of our earthly captivity? Or is it a gospel message ultimately about our need for dependence upon Jesus Christ, our Mediator who himself stood in the gap and accomplished our deliverance?[6]

Jesus before Bethlehem

Esther is the only book in the Bible where God's name isn't mentioned. He's simply nowhere to be found. There are no angelic visitations, either, but there are circumstances that hint that Someone is sovereignly working behind the scenes. For instance, on the very night when the Jews' enemy, Haman, had constructed a gallows on which to hang Mordecai, King Ahasuerus strangely couldn't sleep. "The king just 'happened' to have a sleepless night, and just 'happened' to hear of Mordecai's earlier saving of him! Though we do not have a clear picture of the person of Jesus in the book, we can draw comfort from the truth that even if we don't see him, he is still at work."[7]

Prophecy

Again, there don't seem to be any prophesies about the coming or work of Christ in the book, and that's okay. We don't need to insist that every Old Testament story contain every key we're using to see Jesus. While this book isn't strong on prophetic utterances that point forward to the Lord, it's laced throughout with the gospel story.

Type of Jesus in the Book

As the mediator who risks everything for the sake of her people, Esther is a perfect type of Christ. In her own Gethsemane, she says, "If I perish, I perish" (Esther 4:16), echoing Christ's "Not as I will, but as you will" (Matthew 26:39). In case we start thinking that the point of the book is for us to be like Esther, however, we need to remember that unlike our Savior, "Esther had to be threatened with destruction before she would act," though when she decides to, "the disgraced Jewish girl is about to be used of God to deliver his people."[8]

"By his own merciful initiative, God delights to raise up deliverers for his people when they need him most (1 Corinthians 1:27–28)."[9] And sometimes those deliverers need a little prodding—like both Moses and Esther did. We can be thankful that the Lord Jesus never needed this sort of threat to sacrificially act in love on our behalf. His words weren't "If I perish, I perish," for he knew that he would, indeed, die, and not only that, he would be forsaken by the Father he loved. His love was so great that he "for the joy that was set before him endured the cross" and thought nothing of the shame that attended it (Hebrews 12:2). Through this act of love he has been exalted to God's right hand.

Gospel Story

The treachery of someone like Haman, who cunningly schemed to annihilate an entire race of people, is nothing new. From the very beginning, the Serpent has sought again and again to destroy God's people, but God honored his covenant and preserved the lineage of the Seed of the woman so that we would have life through his death (John 10:10–14). Though we might not see his hand, God is at work even in circumstances that seem hopeless and doomed. And while it is true that the battle will rage until Jesus our conquering King returns to wreak final vengeance upon his and our enemies, we can always be assured that the Lord can be trusted, and that his mercy and provision will continue, even when it appears that we're on the brink of disaster.

Because Jesus (and Esther) stepped into the gap to risk all for their people, we can be assured that we, too, will have "light and gladness and joy and honor" (Esther 8:16) and will shout and rejoice at his return.

Esther teaches us that human weakness is the channel through which divine power is manifested. "The gospel truth is given its richest meaning in Jesus, who won the greatest victory of all just when his enemies thought they had vanquished him (Colossians 2:14–15)."[10]

Not Morality Tales

There are a lot of studies about these Bible characters that use them as a way to enjoin us to be like them. Be courageous like Deborah. Be . . . (what?) like Esther? Bold! (Let's skip the part about being "married" to a pagan king.) Again, while it isn't wrong to look at the lives of women of faith in the Bible and seek to emulate the good things they do, that's not the primary reason these stories are there. They are there to help us see, anticipate, and worship Jesus. As we learn the lessons that Jesus taught his friends, beginning on the Emmaus road, we, too, will be able to see his suffering and his glory everywhere.

Open Bible, Open Heart

1. Have you ever thought about these stories in the light of Jesus and the gospel?

----

2. Hebrews 12:2 reminds us that "Jesus, the founder and per- fecter of our faith, who for the joy that was set before him endured the cross, despising the shame, and is seated at the right hand of the throne of God." How do the stories of Deborah, Ruth, and Esther speak about the gospel message of suffering before glory?

_____

_____

_____

_____

3. How would viewing their stories as "morality tales" obscure that message?

_____

_____

_____

_____

4. In four or five sentences, summarize what you've learned in this chapter.

_____

_____

_____

_____

FOR FURTHER STUDY

1. Choose one other story that you're familiar with in the history books and see if you can find Jesus there (it doesn't need to be about a woman, but it could be).

2. For example, read the story of Abigail (beginning in 1 Samuel 25) and see if you can discern the gospel there. Remember, we don't want to try to make connections where there are

none, but we do want to see the ones that are there. As a reminder, our four categories are

a. Jesus before Bethlehem

b. Prophecy

c. Types of Jesus in the passage

d. How is the gospel story told here?

_____

_____

_____

3. As you do these studies, are you beginning to experience a new zeal or excitement about the gospel as you see it in the Old Testament? _____

5

Finding the Love of Jesus in His Songs and Sayings

"For I know that my Redeemer lives,
and at the last he will stand upon the earth."

Job 19:25

Now that we've looked at the history of redemption as seen in a few of the stories of the women of Israel, let's see where we can discover the good news in a different kind of writing, that is, in poetry and wisdom literature. Here we'll learn how to discover Jesus and the good news in these six books: Job, Psalms, Proverbs, Ecclesiastes, Song of Solomon, and Lamentations, and we'll learn how to read this genre in the way Jesus meant for us to read it.

Finding Jesus' Love in Job's Suffering

Most Christians don't know quite what to do with the book of Job. Part of that has to do with its genre: It's a poetic dialogue with strange, ancient references. So perhaps it would be easier to read Job if we read it like the script of a play, which is what it most closely resembles. There are some beginning and ending narratives setting the stage for the opening dialogue and bringing it to a close, but it's mostly a conversation among five people. It's not easy to read the script of a play, especially when it's written like ancient poetry.

It's also hard to read and understand Job because the topics represented there are both dark and confusing. If it's true, as Job 1:1, 8, 22, and 2:3 say, that Job was a supremely righteous man, then why would God allow Satan to ravage him? Is Job an innocent sufferer, as he claims, or is God punishing him for unbelief because he "feared" that something like this would come upon him? (Job 3:25).[1] Or is there something else happening here? Is there a "deeper magic,"[2] as C. S. Lewis put it? Perhaps we shy away from Job because there aren't any obvious moral lessons or practical steps to be implemented. What five steps could we cull from Job's suffering that would enable us to live carefree lives? And then, of course, maybe it's not our favorite book because we'd like to shy away from Job's life story no matter how it ends. Wouldn't it be easier to pretend that nothing this confusing or devastating ever happens? Let's think now about how we might read the book, keeping Jesus' Easter Sunday lesson in view.

Jesus before Bethlehem

Where might we find Jesus at work in this book? He is the One who speaks astounding wisdom to Job from a whirlwind. He is the Creator who asks, "Where were you when I laid the foundation of the earth?" (Job 38:4). In this one question, he shuts the mouths of those who think they've got the quid pro quo thing all figured out. He is the One who overrules all our "wisdom" and turns all our self-righteous opinions upside down. Job needed to have his understanding expanded; he needed to see that his philosophy of works-righteousness was false, so the Lord crushed him beneath a mountain of wisdom in much the same way Jesus did when he taught that everyone, even those who appear blessed, need mercy and forgiveness. (See Mark 10:23–24.)

Prophetic Words about Jesus

About halfway through the book, Job finally begins to turn slowly away from his own defense and toward hope in God alone. Although Job may not have perceived that it was actually Jesus the Messiah he was talking about, Christians everywhere have taken his words and applied them to their own suffering and hope for their own resurrection and eternal comfort. Job wishes that he could record these words forever . . . and in the Scripture he has:

> "For I know that my Redeemer lives,
> and at the last he will stand upon the earth.
> And after my skin has been thus destroyed,
> yet in my flesh I shall see God,
> whom I shall see for myself,
> and my eyes shall behold, and not another.
> My heart faints within me!"
>
> Job 19:25–27

Job rightly identifies the Lord as his Redeemer, the one who will ultimately free him from all his suffering and oppression. But he also references events yet to come, events that won't have their ultimate fulfillment until Jesus' return and our ultimate resurrection when we will stand, once again, on the earth in physical bodies with eyes that see him. Then we will, as Paul wrote, see him "face to face" (1 Corinthians 13:12).

Type of Jesus

Job is an innocent (though not sinless) sufferer. Jesus, on the other hand, was a completely sinless sufferer, who bore all God's wrath for our sin in his own body.

> He committed no sin, neither was deceit found in his mouth. When he was reviled, he did not revile in return; when he suffered, he did not threaten, but continued entrusting himself to him who judges justly. He himself bore our sins in his body on the tree.
>
> 1 Peter 2:22–24

No one ever suffered like Jesus did. He was completely innocent and didn't demand to preserve his reputation like Job did, but instead laid aside his reward for righteousness for us: "Like a lamb that is led to the slaughter . . . so he opened not his mouth" (Isaiah 53:7).

Gospel Story

The book of Job teaches us that Christianity is not a meritocracy (though that would make it easier to understand) and God is not a cosmic vending machine. All four of the leading characters in this play were mistaken. Job's three friends thought there was no such thing as undeserved suffering. On the other hand, Job was living it and couldn't understand why God had singled him out for such pain. He knew that he didn't have any skeletons in his closet, and yet couldn't square that truth with his ongoing suffering. This book, and the gospel, demonstrate that the world doesn't run on a quid pro quo—"what goes around comes around"—kind of karma. Thankfully, grace stops what goes around from coming back around on us. Though unsettling, the ways of the Lord are meant to comfort and free us.

James wrote, "You have heard of the steadfastness of Job, and you have seen the purpose of the Lord, how the Lord is compassionate and merciful" (James 5:11). That God is compassionate and merciful is the primary message of the gospel, not the quid pro quo of karma. James uses Job as an example of a steadfast sufferer, but he also tells us that his story portrays the "purpose of the Lord."

How does this book teach us about the Lord's compassion and mercy? You'll remember that Job's suffering began when Satan challenged God's goodness by alleging that the only reason Job served him was because God was his Sugar Daddy. The Lord's purpose was to silence Satan's insidious assertion by proving that Job served him because of God's gracious character, not because he had made him rich. And that is one of the main lessons we can learn from this book: The more we know about God's compassion and mercy, the more we'll be motivated to serve him. The gospel is the fuel that's meant to empower our diligence throughout our entire life, even through times of terrible suffering. Job tells us that the wisdom of God is beyond our comprehension, but even so, we have nothing to fear.

Finding the Love of Jesus in His People's Songs

The Psalms were Jesus' hymnal; they were his playlist. Imagine him as a little boy, learning the songs from his parents, struggling with the language and yet desiring in his innocent heart to worship Yahweh. As time went on and his voice and self-understanding grew stronger, he loved to sing God's praises with God's people. "I will tell of your name to my brothers; in the midst of the congregation I will sing your praise" (Hebrews 2:12) is written of him. He knew he was the One who would one day lead all of Israel in worship. During his life, Jesus sang these songs to himself, so much so that even when he hung in agony on the cursed tree, he sang one of them out to his Father, "My God, my God, why have you forsaken me?" (Psalm 22:1; Matthew 27:46).

Jesus said he could be found specifically in the Psalter (Luke 24:44). So if we read the Psalms as though they're primarily about us and how we should pray and sing, we've missed the point. The Psalms are not primarily about us (though we find our hearts resonating with them all the time). They are about Jesus and how he fulfills every one of his people's cries: cries for help, strength, wisdom, faithfulness, thanksgiving, trust, deliverance, joy, and relationship. Reading them without remembering him is to fail to read them aright. So when we read them we should ask

- what might this song have meant to Jesus when he sang it?
- how does it speak to my heart as one who has been forgiven of sin and now stands as a beloved daughter before the Father?

We would also do well to remember that the Psalms are foremost music for God's people to sing and pray. They are lyrics to a song, musical poetry, so we shouldn't interpret them woodenly. For instance, when David writes, "You have . . . put my tears in your bottle. Are they not in your book?" (Psalm 56:8), we shouldn't interpret that to mean that God has a big jar up in heaven where all our tears are collected. Rather, this poetry is meant to reassure us that God sees and remembers all our suffering, and therefore we can proclaim, "God is for me" (v. 9).

Jesus before Bethlehem

Psalm 1 is well known for enjoining trust in God and his Word and the good that comes to those whose "delight is in the law of the Lord" (Psalm 1:2). This psalm teaches us about the blessings that accrue to those who meditate on his Word and assures us that the Lord "knows the way of the righteous" (v. 6).

How does this psalm show us Jesus before his incarnation? Obviously, he is the one who delighted in and meditated on God's Word "day and night." In fact, he spent so much time in the Scriptures that he nearly unconsciously quoted them, especially during his times of trial.[3] Like the "blessed" man's, his life produced luscious fruit, and he prospered in the work his Father had sent him to do. So, is Psalm 1 primarily an encouragement about the blessing of reading and praying faithfully? Of course, it is most certainly that, but that's not all it is. For if we read it without remembering Jesus, then the disturbing turn of events on Good Friday won't make any sense to us. This Psalm not only tells us of the blessing of the righteous and the punishment of the wicked but it also brings us good news, seen in the contrast between promised blessing and Jesus' life experience. Did Jesus fail to delight in God's law? Why doesn't he look like a lush tree instead of the chaff that the "wind drives away" (Psalm 1:3–4)? Rather, this psalm teaches us the "deeper magic," the truth that Jesus is the perfectly Righteous Man of Psalm 1 who suffers at the hands of scoffing sinners so that we might be granted his record of righteousness and thus be motivated to love and delight in God's law.

Prophetic Words That Point to Christ

Since Jesus is the "Word made flesh" (John 1:14), he is the ultimate source of every psalm. When David and the other writers penned these words, they were being inspired by the Spirit of Christ to express their emotions to a Father who loved and welcomed them. Jesus himself was so familiar with them that he quoted the Psalms verbatim at least fifteen times as being specifically about him. The New Testament writers also alluded to Jesus being the fulfillment of the Psalms many, many times. Specifically during the hours of his death, they wrote that he fulfilled more than two dozen prophecies.[4] He is the suffering and rejoicing obedient Son of Psalm 22, who speaks with his Father about everything and trusts him in all things. And he is the One who agonizes in our place.

Type and Gospel Theme

Because these psalms were not only sung by the God-Man Jesus but also composed by the preincarnate Christ, we can rest assured that every sort of lament, complaint, doubt, plea, and song of rejoicing is safe for us to employ. Jesus prayed these prayers. He sang these songs. And he did so with perfect motives and in true faith. Because of this we can know that every one of the Psalms' injunctions to trust in God have been perfectly fulfilled by our Savior while he also took upon himself all of our sinful complaints and unbelief. He leads us as the church's choir director, and the Father invites us to sing with and to him with abandon as he fulfills his role as both our High Priest who leads us and the sacrifice for sin that makes it possible for us to come into his presence.

Finding the Love of Jesus in His Wisdom

At first glance, it appears that the Proverbs are only wise sayings that declare truth about the general grain of the world, the best ways to live, and the difference between foolishness and wisdom. In them we find a "gracious offer of divine wisdom for foolish and weak people."[5] But that's not all we find there. As we're about to see, they are also a demonstration of the gospel.

As a side note, since Proverbs is part of the poetic section of the Bible, we have to be careful in how literally we read it. It should not be read woodenly, as though there weren't any poetic metaphors there, nor should we read it like words from a promise box. The Proverbs are true representations of how life in this world is best lived, but they are only that. They don't promise that our lives will always turn out the way we hope.

Jesus before Bethlehem

Jesus is the epitome of the wise son who attends carefully to his father's counsel. Over and over again, Proverbs presents us with a father's appeal to his son to be wise, so it's not surprising that is exactly how Jesus is described in both his childhood and as an adult. As a young child, Jesus "grew and became strong, filled with wisdom" (Luke 2:40), and at age twelve the teachers were "amazed at his understanding and his answers" (Luke 2:47). Not only did he know the right thing to do, he also did it—even as a child, after he had become aware of his true identity. Jesus "went down with [his parents] and came to Nazareth and was submissive to them" (Luke 2:51).

Imagine: God submitted to flawed human parents. But Jesus isn't merely the wise son who should expect to be blessed; he also represents the foolish son whose back received blows and scourging. Where do we see Jesus in Proverbs? We see him receiving condemnation and beatings reserved for scoffers and fools (Proverbs 19:29; Matthew 27:26). In light of Proverbs' words about blessing for the wise son and condemnation for the fool, it's no wonder that Mary and Cleopas (and the rest of the disciples) were so confused. Why would God allow his wise Son to be beaten like a fool? Was God unfair? Was Jesus unwise? Were the Scriptures false? The horrific events of Good Friday simply won't make sense if we read the Proverbs as promises or simple moral injunctions with promises attached.

Prophetic Words That Speak of Jesus

Where do we hear Jesus' voice speaking in Proverbs? He is the voice of wisdom in Proverbs 8. Although this beautiful passage speaks with a female voice, as wisdom was always depicted in the Ancient Near East, it is certainly his voice that invites us, the simple, to become wise:

> Take my instruction instead of silver,
> > and knowledge rather than choice gold,
> for wisdom is better than jewels,
> > and all that you may desire cannot compare with her.
> > > Proverbs 8:10-11

Don't those verses remind you of Jesus' words in Matthew 16:26: "For what will it profit a man if he gains the whole world and forfeits his soul? Or what shall a man give in return for his soul?"

As the voice of Wisdom, Jesus reminisces about the early days of creation when he walked in the garden of Eden, joyfully communing with his creation:

> And I was daily his delight,
>> rejoicing before him always,
>> rejoicing in his inhabited world
>>> and delighting in the children of man.
>>>> Proverbs 8:30–31

Paul identified Jesus' mission as the very personification of wisdom: Christ crucified is not only the power of God but *also* the wisdom of God (1 Corinthians 1:24, 30), a wisdom that has become ours. He even goes so far as to say that in Christ "are hidden all the treasures of wisdom and knowledge" (Colossians 2:3).

Type of Jesus and the Gospel

Proverbs 31 is often used to bid women to become "excellent" wives. Again, it is not wrong for us to read these words looking for wisdom in our daily lives. But would that be how Jesus read them? As a young man did he take these words as a way to judge which women would qualify for entrance into his royal family? Aside from his mother, Mary, it doesn't seem like it. Were the women who followed him known for their excellent character? Well, not really.

Instead, perhaps we should read this proverb as Jesus' description of his bride. Because he loves us the way he does, this is how he sees us. That isn't because he's like a doting old grandfather who can't see any wrong in his granddaughter. No, it's because he

95

knows that he has fulfilled this entire description of excellence and has clothed us with this righteousness (Isaiah 61:10). He is the trustworthy one who does us good and not harm. He arose while it was still night and provided food for his household. He considered the cost to buy the field of this world and he bought it with his own life. He opened his hand to the poor and needy and clothes us all with scarlet. And he viewed the days before him with joy, knowing that our wedding day was fast approaching.

Gospel Theme

Proverbs is a book of wisdom. A woman who wants to become wise will read it carefully and take its maxims to heart. It is to be read as the original readers would have: as the way of life that would bring blessing from a faithful God. We must never ignore the obvious original intent. But we must also see it in a deeper way, in the way that the Lord and the writers of the New Testament did. Jesus claimed that he was the one who would repay a man according to his work (Proverbs 24:12; Matthew 16:27) and who was the example of a righteous man who didn't give up when he was tried (Proverbs 3:11; Hebrews 12:3).

But where do we find the gospel in Proverbs? In Proverbs, we discover the good news that though we are frequently foolish, though we may have ignored our parents' instruction, or failed to work diligently or to always live wisely, we don't receive the judgment that we deserve. Jesus is the only One who always lived as a Wise Son, and yet the reward for his faithfulness is given to us. Proverbs forces us to a deeper wisdom, one that sees a wise, God-honoring Son receive blows meant for rebellious fools.

> But we impart a secret and hidden wisdom of God, which God decreed before the ages for our glory. None of the rulers of this

age understood this, for if they had, they would not have crucified the Lord of glory.

1 Corinthians 2:7–8

This kind of wisdom had been hidden from the powerful,
the worldly wise, the strong, the popular, the pious, those "together" holier-than-thou overachievers who might want to post
catchy Proverbs around the house so they can give themselves
Good job! stickers with aplomb. The gospel isn't meant for those
who continue to view themselves in this way. It will disgust
them. It is meant for the weak and the sick, for the outcast,
the sinner, the stranger, the unclean, and those who come
with nothing in their hands.[6] In other words, it's meant for you
and me.

The Gospel according to Solomon

The final two books of poetic literature are Ecclesiastes and Song
of Solomon. In Ecclesiastes, we read the musings of Solomon, a
man who has everything except the gospel when he first begins
to write. He looks at the world and it doesn't make sense—he
sees it as pointless and chaotic, which, of course, it is, unless
you see it through the lens of the gospel. "Our search for eternal
life, rest, joy, and justice moves us beyond creation's . . . futility
to Christ."[7] It is only when we view both the Scriptures and the
world through the lens of the good news that even seemingly
meaningless suffering makes sense.

The Song of Solomon is essentially a love song between a
husband and wife. It has been interpreted in many ways down
through church history. In earlier times, when open talk about
sex was frowned upon, it was almost always allegorized as being

words between Christ and his bride, the church. In these days, however, no one has any problem speaking publicly about even the most private matters, so it is now almost exclusively taken as a sex manual for couples. While not bypassing its literal meaning, my friend Dr. Iain Duguid wrote this in his commentary:

> The Song of Songs speaks to us of Christ and the gospel precisely as it speaks to us concerning human love and marriage. As it confronts us with the ideal of such love, it convicts each of us of our personal sin and failure, and shows us our need of redemption. The Song challenges all of us as failed lovers and points us to the perfect Lover, who has loved us and given himself for us.[8]

The Gospel in All the Songs and Sayings

I hope that you're now beginning to understand why Jesus claimed that the Old Testament was about him. But that's not all I'm hoping for. I'm hoping that as you're beginning to understand that truth, your heart is warming up to reading his Word as you anticipate finding the One who loves you so perfectly.

As you now read about the outwardly blameless sufferer, Job, I hope you'll be reminded of our completely innocent Savior. Has his story taken on new meaning for you?

Does the fact that Jesus wrote, prayed, and sang the Psalms embolden you to approach your Father, freely expressing the entire range of human emotion, knowing that Jesus has already prayed them perfectly in your place and opened the door for you to sing your way into the throne room of heaven where we may "receive mercy and find grace to help in time of need" (Hebrews 4:16)?

And does the truth of the wise Son who received blows intended for fools encourage you to read the Proverbs and seek to apply them in practical ways in your life, knowing that even when you fail you're still counted as wise?

This is how reading the Old Testament while remembering the gospel can transform your desire to read Scripture, because it is in that reading you'll be able to see how deeply and faithfully you are loved, and you'll begin to see the face of the One who has loved you from the beginning of time.

OPEN BIBLE, OPEN HEART

1. Have you ever read the book of Job? If so, what did you think of it? If you haven't, is there a specific reason why you haven't?

   _____

   _____

   _____

2. Have you read through the Psalms? If so, do you have a favorite psalm? For instance, many people love Psalm 23. Why do you think that is?

   _____

   _____

   _____

3. Have you ever read the Proverbs? Are there particular verses that speak to you? Which ones in particular?

   _____

   _____

   _____

4. Look back over what you've just written. Are you beginning to see the songs and sayings in a different light? In what

way? Now do you feel more inclined to read through them in the hope that you'll find good news there?

5. Summarize what you've learned in this chapter in four or five sentences.

For Further Study

1. Read one psalm of your choice. Without ignoring the original meaning of it, and without drawing analogies that aren't plain, can you see the gospel in it?

2. Read Ecclesiastes, Song of Solomon, or Lamentations and try to find the gospel there. You can do so by remembering the categories we've used and by asking these questions:

   a. How does this book demonstrate our need for a Redeemer?

   b. How does this book demonstrate that Jesus is the kind of Redeemer we need?

6

Finding the Love of Jesus in His Prophets

> The prophets . . . prophesied about the grace that was
> to be yours. . . . It was revealed to them that they were
> serving not themselves but you.
>
> 1 Peter 1:10, 12

One of the most fascinating (and frequently confusing) sections of the Scriptures is that of the prophetic books found at the end of the Old and New Testaments. There are seventeen in the Old, from Isaiah to Malachi, and one in the New, the Revelation of John, written by Jesus' best friend, John.

Learning to properly interpret the writings of the prophets is a skill that Jesus taught his disciples after his resurrection. Jesus himself believed that the words of the prophets were words about him.

In order to rightly interpret the prophetic books, we need to learn several things: To begin with, we should try to understand what these prophecies meant to those who originally heard them. Was the prophet warning them because they were living in sin?

Or was the prophet foretelling times of blessing that would come? If you have a study Bible, prophetic passages are frequently cross-referenced to events in the nation of Israel, making the first step of right interpretation easy.[1]

Second, we need to try to discover where the prophet pointed to the Messiah. Jesus himself said that certain events in his life took place so that "the Scriptures of the prophets might be fulfilled" (Matthew 26:56). He was confident that he was the ultimate fulfillment of Old Testament prophecies, and so were the writers of the New Testament.[2]

I know it seems pretty obvious to us on this side of Calvary that Isaiah 53:5—"But he was pierced for our transgressions; he was crushed for our iniquities"—refers to Jesus, but Isaiah's original readers didn't have that perspective. We know that because it was a shock to the disciples that the role of the Crushed One would be fulfilled by their Messiah. Rather, they thought he was there to crush their Gentile oppressors. But once they learned how to interpret the prophets, they were able to make right connections from them to him.[3]

The Infallible Interpreters

Sometimes the links between the Old Testament prophets and New Testament events are fairly easy to see. For instance, Isaiah 29:18:

> In that day the deaf shall hear
>   the words of a book,
> and out of their gloom and darkness
>   the eyes of the blind shall see.

was used by Jesus himself as words about him. When his cousin John wondered about his identity, Jesus said, "Go and tell John what you have seen and heard: the blind receive their sight, the lame walk, lepers are cleansed, and the deaf hear" (Luke 7:22).

In one of his most audacious claims, Jesus asserted that he was *the* fulfillment of Isaiah's prophecy, in chapter 61. Jesus had gone to the synagogue on the Sabbath and stood up to read. Being given the scroll of Isaiah, he unrolled it, found this place, and read:

> "The Spirit of the Lord is upon me,
>   because he has anointed me
>   to proclaim good news to the poor.
> He has sent me to proclaim liberty to the captives
>   and recovering of sight to the blind,
>   to set at liberty those who are oppressed,
> to proclaim the year of the Lord's favor."
>
> Luke 4:18–19

After reading the passage, Jesus said, "Today this Scripture has been fulfilled in your hearing" (Luke 4:21). In making this proclamation, he was declaring himself to be their long-awaited Messiah. I wonder what he would have done if he had been given a different scroll, say one from Jeremiah or Ezekiel. Would he have been able to find himself in it? Undoubtedly. The prophets were all about him and he could use any of them to prove it.

The apostles also used prophecies to link the Old Testament to the New and assure the church of Christ's identity and their place in his kingdom:

> "Behold, I am the one who has laid as a foundation
>   in Zion,
>   a stone, a tested stone,
> a precious cornerstone, of a sure foundation:
>   'Whoever believes will not be in haste.'"
>
> Isaiah 28:16

This Isaiah passage was used by Paul to speak of Israel's failure to believe in righteousness received by faith alone:

> They have stumbled over the stumbling stone, as it is written, "Behold, I am laying in Zion a stone of stumbling, a rock of offense; and whoever believes in him will not be put to shame."
>
> Romans 9:32–33

Paul used this passage again to promise salvation to all who believe: "For the Scripture says, 'Everyone who believes in him will not be put to shame'" (Romans 10:11). Peter also picked up the same passage to encourage the church that we are made "acceptable to God through Jesus Christ," who is a chosen and precious cornerstone, that "whoever believes in him will not be put to shame" (1 Peter 2:5–6). Think of it: Paul used this passage twice and Peter used it once to make similar, yet different, points.

In prophesying about the Lord's undying love for Israel, Hosea recalls the exodus deliverance from Egypt: "When Israel was a child, I loved him, and out of Egypt I called my son" (Hosea 11:1). Matthew picked up this passage, which was obviously first meant to be about Israel's deliverance from Egyptian slavery, and employed it to speak of the holy family's return to Israel after they had fled to Egypt seeking refuge from Herod's sword:

> And he rose and took the child and his mother by night and departed to Egypt and remained there until the death of Herod. This was to fulfill what the Lord had spoken by the prophet, "Out of Egypt I called my son."
>
> Matthew 2:14–15

As I mentioned earlier, we should never forget to read with the original listeners in mind. Therefore, we often have to hold two sometimes very different meanings in mind at the same time. For example, the prophet Nathan's words to David were originally meant to assure David that the Lord would maintain relationship with his son, Solomon. But the writer to the Hebrews uses this phrase: "I will be to him a father, and he shall be to me a son," to refer to Jesus' exaltation over the angels (see 2 Samuel 7:14 and Hebrews 1:5). Remember that reading with both the original intent and the Messianic fulfillment in mind is not an "either-or" proposition. It is rather a "both-and."

Fulfilled Prophecy

For Christians, one of the primary ways we can be assured of Jesus' true identity is fulfilled prophecy:

> The Bible contains several hundred prophecies relating to the birth, life, ministry, death, resurrection, and future return of Jesus Christ. Almost thirty of them were literally fulfilled in one twenty-four-hour period just prior to His death (e.g., those relating to His betrayal, trial, crucifixion, and burial).[4]

The odds that any one man could have fulfilled even eight prophecies about his death given hundreds of years before would be only 1 in 10^{17}. That's 1 in 100,000,000,000,000,000.[5] Coupled with the resurrection, Jesus' fulfillment of prophecy is a primary proof that he was who he claimed to be.

How the Prophets Speak to Us Today

Now we are finally free to ask how a specific prophecy might apply to us, as members of God's household of faith. As the Word of

God, they are part of the Scripture, which is "breathed out by God and profitable for teaching, for reproof, for correction, and for training in righteousness, that the man of God may be complete, equipped for every good work" (2 Timothy 3:16–17).

They function as warnings to us against unbelief and idolatry or as words of comfort during times of trial, enabling us to grow in our love and application of the gospel. But they shouldn't function as predictors of who might win the presidency or the identity of the Antichrist.

Can you see how neglecting to remember the original intent might lead to a wrong interpretation? Let's remember that we need to think about prophecies as far more than words spoken to us in the twenty-first century; they were first spoken to an ancient people, then interpreted by the Lord's apostles as being about him, and then finally given to us as food for our souls.[6]

Finding the Love of Jesus Spoken through Isaiah

Isaiah stands out as one of the strongest voices of the gospel in the Bible, especially in the final section of the book, from chapters 40–66. In fact, Isaiah 53 is often referred to as the fifth gospel, as it so succinctly describes the suffering and mission of our Savior. Let's look for the good news in a different prophecy, this time from Isaiah 63.

Jesus before Bethlehem

Here we find a beautiful prophecy in which "the angel of his presence" is said to have carried ancient Israel through their wanderings, even through times of rebellion. Isaiah recognized that there was a person, "the angel of his presence," who lovingly saved, redeemed, and carried the Lord's people:

In all their affliction he was afflicted,
     and the angel of his presence saved them;
in his love and in his pity he redeemed them;
          he lifted them up and carried them all the days of
          old.

Isaiah 63:9

To the original readers, this passage reminded them of the cloud and pillar of fire that attended the nation of Israel throughout her wilderness wanderings. It assured them that the Lord loved and pitied them, forgave their sins, and carried them into the promised land. The pillar and cloud were not impersonal atmospheric manifestations. They were actually the Son, the "angel of his presence."

A Type That Spoke of the One to Come

To the writers of the New Testament, this passage would be linked inextricably to Jesus, the One who was afflicted for his people (Isaiah 53:4) and who so loved them that he would bear all their burdens (Romans 15:1–4; Galatians 6:2), redeem them (Titus 3:4–7), and carry them daily on his shoulders (Luke 15:5).

Gospel Theme

Isaiah 63 tells the story of the deliverance of God's people through judgment and mercy. The Lord brings judgment on those who oppress his people, but he forgives and keeps those whom he has called to himself. Christians can rest in God's steadfast love for them even when we fail to live as we should, knowing that Jesus was afflicted in our place so that we would be "lifted up" and "carried" by his grace.

Jesus Speaks His Love to an Exile

The history and words of a faithful exile are recorded in the prophetic book of Daniel. Daniel's stand for righteousness practically begs to be made into a moralistic cartoon or catchy song that would be as welcome in a Jewish synagogue or Mormon congregation as it is in many Sunday schools today. It's nearly impossible to resist the urge to proclaim "Dare to be a Daniel" and to use his life primarily as an example of how to heroically stand against secular forces (and eat vegetarian). But "in doing so we neglect Daniel's own message: God is the hero."[7] Before Jesus' resurrection, the disciples would have bought into this moralistic interpretation and application of the book, but Jesus would stand against using the book in this way. He said that this story was actually about him.

In addition to the narrative portion of the book seeming to be a morality tale, the prophetic part begs for us to employ the Headline Method when reading it. It's very tempting to assume Daniel's vision is about twenty-first-century Western civilization and that we should be able to discover how current events intersect with these prophecies. But Daniel's words aren't about the United States, but about the kingdom of the Son being established in all the earth.

Let's consider one of Daniel's prophecies now, in which he interpreted a dream, and see how it speaks of Jesus' life, work, and kingdom to come. Daniel, an exile who had risen to prominence in King Nebuchadnezzar's empire, both received and interpreted a dream the king had about a coming kingdom. The dream was about a great image that represented important kingdoms of the earth that would be crushed by a stone "cut out by no human hand" (Daniel 2:34). The stone struck the image, destroyed it, and "became a great mountain and filled the whole earth" (v. 35).

Seeing Jesus and the Gospel before Bethlehem in the Prophets

In this prophecy, we read about a living stone, a kingdom that would fill the entire earth, would crush every kingdom that stood in its way, and stand forever. It's not hard to find Jesus in this prophecy because he is that massive stone, the limitless mountain, who rules as King over a glorious kingdom that will stand forever. The angel, Gabriel himself, told Mary that her Son would be "great and will be called the Son of the Most High. . . . and he will reign over the house of Jacob forever, and of his kingdom there will be no end" (Luke 1:32–33).

Paul picked up this theme and described Jesus in words that echo Daniel's. Jesus Christ is the one who is . . .

> seated . . . at his right hand in the heavenly places, far above all rule and authority and power and dominion, and above every name that is named, not only in this age but also in the one to come. And he put all things under his feet and gave him as head over all things to the church, which is his body, the fullness of him who fills all in all.
>
> Ephesians 1:20–23

Can you see how using Daniel to teach morals or interpret headlines misses the glorious truth that is meant to comfort us, especially in times of trial when secular powers threaten to destroy the church? Trying to live like Daniel by refusing to stop praying is a good thing. But it is not the point of the book.

Gospel Theme

Daniel preached the gospel by demonstrating that God's grace comes not only to those who try to live faithfully but also to those who are weak and frail and suffering for their sin. Daniel recognized that God was using him "not because of any wisdom" (Daniel 2:30) he had more than anyone else, but rather that God's message of grace and ultimate triumph over evil comes through broken vessels. The Lord's use of us to bring the whole earth under his lordship does not depend on our self-sufficiency but on his ability to use even the weak for his purposes: "Such is the confidence that we have through Christ toward God. Not that we are sufficient in ourselves to claim anything as coming from us, but our sufficiency is from God" (2 Corinthians 3:4–5).

The gospel assures us that Jesus uses broken vessels, weak jars of clay, to accomplish his purposes. It also assures us that Jesus, who didn't need to be told to dare to be a Daniel, was perfectly faithful to obey all of his Father's will so that the prayer he taught us to pray, "Your kingdom come," would be fulfilled through him. Once we recognize and rejoice in Christ's fulfillment of Daniel's prophecies, we will be motivated to persevere in faithful obedience, even in a dark and godless land.

The Gospel in the Minor Prophets

Within the seventeen books usually categorized as prophetic, there is a subcategory of twelve, commonly referred to as the Minor Prophets.[8] These books are not minor because they are insignificant, but because they are shorter[9] and were collected onto one scroll before the time of Christ. The writers of the New Testament were well acquainted with them and cited them verbatim almost fifty times. For instance, Paul twice used an obscure verse in Habakkuk 2:4, "Behold, his soul is puffed up; it is not upright within him, but the righteous shall live by his faith," to emphasize his primary message that believers are saved by grace through faith rather than by the works they boast in: "For in it [the gospel] the righteousness of God is revealed from faith for faith, as it is written, 'The righteous shall live by faith'" (Romans 1:17). "It is evident that no one is justified before God by the law, for 'The righteous shall live by faith'" (Galatians 3:11).

It would be very easy, if we didn't trust that Paul infallibly interpreted the Old Testament, to puzzle over whether he was right by using Habakkuk in this way or if he was taking too much license. We can be confident, though, that he was following the teaching of the Lord who had revealed it to him, "in order that [he] might preach [the gospel] among the Gentiles" (Galatians 1:11–12, 16) from the Old Testament.

The Gospel according to Zechariah

Zechariah tells us of a vision he had regarding Joshua, a high priest after the Jews returned from exile in Persia (see Ezra 3). Zechariah 3 describes Joshua standing as a defendant in a courtroom with Satan, the prosecuting attorney, standing next to him. Satan was eager to accuse Joshua because of his sin, shown by his filthy clothes. His sin would disqualify him from functioning as a priest who was to remove Israel's guilt through temple sacrifices. But God ruled that Satan's accusations were "out of order" before he even stated them because Joshua has been "chosen and rescued by God."[10] In fact, the angel of the Lord represented him. As the trial closes, Joshua is clothed in clean garments and assured of open access into the Lord's presence.

Jesus before Bethlehem

Where might we find Jesus in this beautiful gospel story of forgiveness and cleansing? Who is the one who protects Joshua and clothes him in "pure vestments" (Zechariah 3:4)? The "angel of the Lord," of course. As the preincarnate Son, Jesus stands in court with his sinful servant Joshua and rebukes Satan. He declares that Joshua is a chosen "brand plucked from the fire" (v. 2) and instructs those standing near him to "remove the filthy garments from him" (v. 4). The angel then declares these beautiful gospel words over him, words that every person who is called to give the gospel to their neighbor (but is all too aware of their inadequacies) longs to hear: "Behold, I have taken your iniquity away from you, and I will clothe you with pure vestments" (v. 4). My sisters, are there any words more glorious? Not only are you forgiven for your sin, you are also dressed in righteousness. Glorious exchange! Our filth for his purity!

Gospel Theme

I doubt that it is necessary for me to point out the gospel message to you in this passage. Imagine Joshua's plight: He had returned to Jerusalem from exile because of idolatry. The once beautiful temple that had been their pride had been razed to the ground, and the sacrifices that assured him of God's forgiveness hadn't been offered in decades. Along with his nation, he had been disqualified and judged, and in his own eyes he stood condemned. But then the angel of the Lord spoke the gospel to him and assured him that on a "single day" (v. 9) the iniquity of the land would be removed by "the Branch," the coming Messiah (v. 8).

Thank God for his indescribable grace and mercy, grace poured out on women who would love and serve him but fear that their sin would disqualify them. Thank God for the Branch who was nailed to a tree so that we might be grafted in. Praise him that our iniquity was dealt with in a single day, a Friday strangely called

"Good." Thank God that all of God's wrath for all of our sin was poured out on the Son who loves us so that we don't need to try to earn God's approval or hope that somehow he will still use us. We are forgiven, clothed, and recommissioned no matter how our Enemy accuses us.

The prophets tell us of this glorious good news, and reading them while keeping this story in mind will cause our hearts to be warmed and encouraged.

Open Bible, Open Heart

1. Read Jeremiah 31:33–34 and Ezekiel 36:26–27 as the gospel promises they are. Respond. Can you find any New Testament passages that are similar?

   _____

   _____

   _____

2. In the book of Daniel, we learn that "God calls every nation that opposes him into judgment and destroys them, although he may allow his purposes to be fulfilled by them for a time."[11] Respond.

   _____

   _____

   _____

3. How do Paul's words in 2 Corinthians 9:9–10 encourage you to know that God uses even the weak to accomplish the goal of establishing his kingdom rule over all the earth?

   _____

   _____

   _____

4. The story of Jonah is often used as a morality lesson. I taught my children to sing "I Don't Want to be a Jonah" when they were little, completely missing the gospel story presented in this book. Are you able to see it, and if so, what is it? (Remember to ask yourself where the message of the gospel is seen in the book and then to compare and contrast the main characters in the book with the main character of the Bible, Jesus Christ.)

_____

_____

_____

5. Summarize what you've learned in this chapter in four or five sentences.

_____

_____

_____

For Further Study

1. Read one of the minor prophets (I love Hosea) and see if you can do the following:

   a. Discern what it meant to its original hearers.

   _____

   _____

   _____

   b. See how Jesus would have interpreted it to be about himself.

   _____

   _____

   _____

c. Discover how it might challenge and/or comfort you in your walk of faith.

_____

_____

_____

7

Finding the Love of Jesus in His Law

"For truly, I say to you, until heaven and earth pass away, not an iota, not a dot, will pass from the Law until all is accomplished."

Matthew 5:18

Phil and I have been married for more than forty years. That, as I like to say, proves there is a God. Phil is a very kind and loving husband, and I'm thankful for his patience and care. Over the years he's expressed his love for me in many ways. Sometimes he just comes right out and says, "Have I told you I love you yet today?" (What a sweetie!) There are also other times that his love for me isn't expressed quite so vocally, like when he faithfully worked every day for decades or took the trash cans out to the street on Thursday nights, or went for a hike with me when he'd probably rather watch Westerns. Sometimes, when I'm having a meltdown about something, I can see him start to say something, then stop himself because he knows I just need to vent at that moment. Then there are other times when he comes to me in all seriousness and says, "Honey, we need to talk about . . ." I'm really thankful for Phil and his love for me. He tells me that he loves me all the time, and sometimes he uses words. I'm trying to learn to detect his love even when it isn't so obvious that I've got a box of See's Bordeaux chocolates on my countertop.

The point of this little illustration is this: Just as Phil expresses his love for me in lots of different ways, Jesus says "I love you" to us in many different ways, too. Sometimes he comes right out and says it: "Greater love has no one than this, that someone lay down his life for his friends. You are my friends if you do what I command you" (John 15:13–14). Other times he lets us search him out, like in the story of Esther, so that we can enjoy the thrill of discovery. And at still other times he asks us to trust his claim that the whole Bible speaks of him even when we're having trouble hearing his voice. At times like that we can trust that the Holy Spirit will eventually enable us to hear him if we just keep walking by faith. The entire Bible is one long letter of love, calling his bride to himself and assuring her of his love. I hope that you're beginning to see him everywhere and that you find his love for you motivating your reading of his Word.

How Should I Respond to What I'm Reading?

In this chapter and the next, I'm going to help you see precious truths that will enable you to understand not only what you're reading but also how you should respond to it. As we have already learned, the Bible isn't primarily a collection of stories about heroes we should emulate. It's about the one Hero who draws us to love and worship him.

We have seen that the Bible is written in differing styles or genres (history, poetry, prophecy, etc.). Now we're going to learn that it is also written with two different purposes. The first purpose is to tell us *what God expects of us*. That's the purpose of what is commonly called "the law." The law tells us what to do. The second purpose is to tell us *what God has done for us*. That purpose is usually referred to as "the gospel" or the "good news." The gospel tells us what God has done. Every part of the Bible declares either the law (what God tells us to do) or the gospel (what God has done for us) . . . and sometimes in the same verse! As you'll soon see, it's really important for us to understand the difference between the law and the gospel when we read, because the law and the gospel are written for different reasons, so we're supposed to respond to them in differing ways. The law isn't good news. In fact, if we read it as seriously as it's meant to be read, its actually pretty bad news. The gospel, on the other hand, is great news! It delivers the news that every demand made by the law has already been fulfilled for us by Jesus Christ.

I know that when you hear the words *law* and *gospel* it is easy to think: *Okay, the law . . . that must be the Ten Commandments, and the gospel is what I read in the first four books of the New Testament. Right?* Well, yes, and no. Yes, the Ten Commandments do contain law and the Gospels (Matthew, Mark, Luke, and John) do contain good news. But, no. The Ten Commandments also contain some good news, and the gospels are full of the law. Here's help: A basic way to distinguish law from gospel is to ask this one simple question: *Who is the subject of the verbs?* In any particular verse or passage are we the ones called to do the action, or has God already done it or promised to do it? Any passage that commands us to act can be thought of as law. Conversely, any passage that talks about God doing the work is gospel. Here is an example: See if you can differentiate between these two categories, law and gospel, from this well-known passage at the beginning of the Ten Commandments:

> And God spoke all these words, saying, "I am the Lord your God, who brought you out of the land of Egypt, out of the house of slavery. You shall have no other gods before me."
>
> Exodus 20:1–3

In this passage, both law and gospel are easily seen. The gospel declares that God speaks to us, that he has claimed us for his own, and that he brought us up out of slavery. Since God is the One doing the action, it's the good news. He communicates with us, is near to us, and rescues us. Can you hear Jesus saying that he loves you even here, in the prelude to the first of the Ten Commandments? Because God has done these things for us, the law then demands complete allegiance to the Lord. "No other gods" is law. It's something we're obligated to do in response to what he's already done.

The Law	The Gospel
"You shall have no other gods before me."	"I am the Lord your God, who brought you out of the land of Egypt, out of the house of slavery."

Here's another example. Where do you see law and gospel in the verses below?

> If then you have been raised with Christ, seek the things that are above, where Christ is, seated at the right hand of God. Set your minds on things that are above, not on things that are on earth. For you have died, and your life is hidden with Christ in God.

When Christ who is your life appears, then you also will appear with him in glory.

Colossians 3:1–4

The Law	The Gospel
"Seek the things that are above. Set your minds on things that are above, not on things that are on earth."	"You have been raised with Christ, who is seated at God's right hand. You have died, and your life is hidden with Christ in God. You will appear with Christ in glory. He is your life."

In these verses, we are the subject of the verbs twice: We are to seek and set our minds on the things that are above. The law in this passage is *seek* and *set*. We are being commanded to do something. On the other hand, the good news or gospel in this passage is that we have been raised with Christ, are seated at the right hand of God, our old life is gone, and the life that empowers us now is the very life of Christ, with whom we are hidden in God, and because of that we will appear with Jesus in glory. It's pretty encouraging to see all the work God has done for us in Christ, right? Have you ever read that passage and rejoiced because you're loved like that?

Realizing that we've been loved and provided for in such a marvelous way will motivate us to seek him and set our affection on him, all in response to what he's already done. He says, "I love you this much," to which you reply, "I want to know you and think about you all the time." That's how the good news and our response work together. The law and the gospel are partners in bringing us closer to him. He promises that he's done everything for us, and we respond by desiring and seeking after him.

Are you beginning to see how insufficient it would be for us to read over the verses above and only pay attention to what we're supposed to be doing? I admit that formerly that's how I would have read those passages. I would read that glorious good news about Jesus' love and come away thinking, "I've got to do a better job of seeking and setting. I need to kill all my idols." And while those two statements are true, they don't have the power to motivate me to obey. Only the recognition of what he's already done for me will motivate me to fight to know him and abandon all my false gods. Conversely, if we only think about what God has done for us and never about how we should respond, we're missing half the message. God has given us both the law and the gospel. And we need them both.

The law, though from God and thoroughly good and holy, has a completely different function than the gospel, and surprisingly, its function isn't to make us good enough for God to love us. The law can't do that because a command doesn't give us the strength to obey it. It only tells us what God expects from us. The gospel's declarations, on the other hand, infuse us with motivation and power to obey what the law commands. Both the law and the gospel are necessary for the Christian to hear. Both are good, and good for us. And both are to be believed and taken to heart.

The Three Uses of the Law

The rest of this chapter will be devoted to unpacking the purpose of the law—what it's meant to do—more clearly. Then in the next chapter we'll hear more about the good news, what God has already done for us, the gospel.

In the past, wise people who loved God developed a way to talk about the law, the commands God has given. They said that there were three uses for it. The first use is to bring everyone under

God's judgment and declare the whole world guilty. The second use is to remind everyone, even non-Christians, about the right way to live. And the third use is to guide believers in the way of gratitude (what we've just been talking about).

Let's apply these three uses of the law to a well-known conversation Jesus had with a lawyer. The lawyer asked Jesus to choose the greatest commandment. Jesus answered, "You shall love the Lord your God with all your heart and with all your soul and with all your mind. This is the great and first commandment" (Matthew 22:37–38).

First Use of the Law

If you read that command with even an ounce of self-awareness, you'd know that you've not obeyed it. You may want to love God, you may try to love him, you may even pray that he helps you. But the command isn't to *try* to love; it is to do it, with *all* your heart, soul, and mind. You either love him supremely, at all times, above all things, or you don't. And here's the truth (if you're willing to admit it), you don't. Neither do I. No one (aside from Jesus) ever has. Perhaps you're having trouble agreeing with that statement, so here's help: Have you ever been angry because you didn't get something you wanted? At that very moment, you were placing your desires (what you wanted) above the love and worship of your Creator. You've broken the first commandment. Or, have you ever felt sorry for yourself because others have more than you do or proud because you thought you were better than others? If so, you're guilty of breaking God's primary law.[1]

God commands that my love for him overrule every other love in my life. And he doesn't grade on a curve (and if he did, Jesus ruined it!). In God's courtroom, we are either guilty or innocent. We get a pass or a fail. There isn't a "nice try" category. And because we, all of us, love ourselves and other things more than we love God, we all fail. We are all guilty. We all stand condemned. And that, my sisters, is the first use of the law. It's meant to let you know that you don't have any intrinsic self-righteousness to rely on before a perfect and holy God, who sees not only your outward actions but also the inner motivations of your heart: "And no creature is hidden from his sight, but all are naked and exposed to the eyes of him to whom we must give account" (Hebrews 4:13).

God has made one simple demand: Love me the most. We have failed utterly. Can you see how desperately we need Someone to rescue us? We all need a Savior, but before we come to understand and really feel our need, we have to accept the fact that we are guilty lawbreakers. That is why Paul wrote "None is righteous, no, not one" (Romans 3:10) when he was laying out the gospel. He knew we needed to see our problem before we would be ready to accept God's solution.

So then, the first use of the law is to crush our self-righteousness and force us to look for salvation from a source outside of ourselves. Paul, a man who knew and loved the law, wrote that the law kills (2 Corinthians 3:6). He called it a ministry of death that brought condemnation (vv. 7, 9). The law would bring us life and righteousness if we obeyed it. But since we don't, it can't: "For if a law had been given that could give life, then righteousness would indeed be by the law" (Galatians 3:21).

Salvation can't come to us by obedience to the law because no one obeys it—not from pure motives, not every nanosecond of every day that you breathe God's air. No one.

It is in this way that through the law Jesus says to us "I love you." He frees us from the tyranny of trying to work our way to heaven. He tells us, *You can't do it. Give up and die to your own righteousness and trust me.* And that, though it seems strange, is a very loving thing for Jesus to say to us. In fact, it's the only way we will ever know any joy or rest.[2]

Second Use of the Law

The second purpose of the law is to act as a restraint on society in general. Everyone, even the unbeliever, recognizes that they are not supposed to live their lives as though they were the center of the universe. Even people who don't believe in the God of the Bible know that proud, selfish, bragging god-imposters are awful to be around. The iconic movie *Groundhog Day*[3] resonates with audiences because it proves this point. No one likes Bill Murray's character, Phil Connors, until finally he becomes a person who loves other people and realizes that he isn't God. Why? Because "no other gods" is written on the conscience of every person (Romans 2:15–16). In this way, the law helps curb (at least outwardly) the innate selfishness of all people, believers and unbelievers.

Some people think all moral law is merely a product of what a society has come to believe is acceptable behavior and there isn't any law that comes from outside of us, from God. But the truth is there is uniformity in every society that demonstrates there are fundamental rules resident in every person's conscience. For instance, there isn't any society where selling one's six-year-old daughter into sexual slavery is okay (though it is done). There isn't any society where stealing another man's wife is approved. No society elevates a man who gleefully robs, rapes, and murders his own mother. In fact, you can pretty much go through the entire Ten Commandments and find that they still function as a restraint on the innate selfishness and self-love of all people.

That's the second function of the law, and it's a good thing. It speaks of Jesus' love for us because a society of laws and justice is a good (though not perfect) place to live. Because we are all curved in on ourselves, all humanity needs to be restrained. But this restraint can only reach so far. No member of any society obeys all the law perfectly, which is why all societies have a court system that protects victims and punishes evildoers (see Romans 13:1–5). And no society can earn its way into God's favor by perfect obedience . . . because no society perfectly obeys.

Third Use of the Law[4]

The third use of the law is *only* for the Christian. Its function is what we talked about at the opening of this chapter. This use is for the one who has tasted of God's sweet grace and forgiveness and wants to respond in grateful obedience. In this case, the law reminds us that we should love God because he has already loved us. It makes us grateful that Jesus perfectly obeyed all the law in our place, and because he did, we long to respond in kind. What this third use should *not* do, however, is cause us to think that our grateful obedience earns God's love for us. So, should we strive to love in response to his love? Yes, of course. But whatever we accomplish in our striving, none of it merits God's love or care for us. We can't be good enough, but he loves us anyway.

In this use, the law functions to awaken me from my self-deception, apathy, and pride. For instance, when I read this law: "Be kind to one another, tenderhearted, forgiving one another . . ."

(Ephesians 4:32), the Holy Spirit uses it as a prod to remind me that I need to seek to put off my selfish demanding and lack of forgiveness, and instead ask the Lord for a tender heart that generously accepts and welcomes fellow sinners.

Because I am a Christian who has been forgiven for all my sin and who is now indwelt by the Holy Spirit, I desire to strive with all the strength that is in me to love and forgive my neighbor. I am glad that there are days when I can see God is working this change of heart in me, and I'm thankful for his grace and patience. But there are also days when I'm not sure I've ever really forgiven anyone at all, and again I'm thankful for his grace and patience.

On both those days, the third use of the law calls on me to respond in faith: not to try to *earn* God's favor and love, *but because I already have it*. On the days when I actually do forgive an enemy, I can continue to rest in the knowledge that it was God who accomplished this work in me and not my own goodness (Ephesians 2:10). And on other days, when I fail, I need to remember that my obedience to God's law isn't what has opened his heart of love for me and that my failure, though grievous, won't close his heart to me, either. Paul wrote, "While we were enemies we were reconciled to God by the death of his Son, much more, now that we are reconciled, shall we be saved by his life" (Romans 5:10).

If we were reconciled to God by the death of his Son while we were enemies, he will certainly keep us, even on the days when we really struggle. In fact, when we're really struggling and needing loads of help, he commands us to come to him: "Let us then with confidence draw near to the throne of grace, that we may receive mercy and find grace to help in time of need" (Hebrews 4:16).

Can you see how even my failure to obey might ultimately make me thankful that Jesus has loved me in spite of my failure and grateful that my salvation isn't based on my own growth in godliness? If it were, then I wouldn't have any assurance of salvation or even of Jesus' never-failing love because my obedience is never what it should be. *The good news is that God's love for me isn't based on me at all.* All of it is based on Jesus' work on my behalf, and though that's the message of the gospel, even the law forces us to seek it out. The law speaks of Jesus' love for us even when it convicts us for failing to obey it.

So, how should we respond when we find that once again we've failed to love? We should admit our failure and then trust that God's love never fails. We can say with confidence:

> I acknowledged my sin to you,
>> and I did not cover my iniquity;
> I said, "I will confess my transgressions to the Lord,"
>> and you forgave the iniquity of my sin.
>
> Psalm 32:5

The law is good for the Christian because it reminds us of our need for Jesus, the One who is ever waiting to welcome us, and because it shows us how to respond in gratitude to the One who has loved us. We never need to fear coming to the Lord in our brokenness. Remember, Jesus is the One who was known as the Friend of Sinners (Matthew 11:19).

As you grow in your ability to distinguish between the law and the gospel, remembering the three ways the law is used, you'll find that the message of the Bible will become more and more clear. In the next chapter, we'll spend time unpacking the good news that is the only true motivation for obeying the law. Remember that the primary law is to love, and love is always responsive in nature. He loves us, therefore we love him and want to please him. Only as you remember how much he has loved you will you be motivated to love and obey in return.

Open Bible, Open Heart

1. What's an easy way to tell the difference between the law and the gospel?

_____

_____

_____

_____

2. What are the three uses of the law? Have you ever thought about God's rules in this way before? How does this way of thinking help you?

_____

_____

_____

_____

3. How does the first use of the law, to bring everyone under God's guilty verdict, speak to us of Jesus' love for us?

_____

_____

_____

_____

4. What is the problem facing everyone that the law forces us to see? How is this a good thing?

_____

_____

_____

_____

_____

5. How should the third use of the law, to show us how to respond in grateful obedience, function in our lives? What should it *not* do?

_____

_____

_____

_____

6. Summarize what you've learned in this chapter in four or five sentences.

_____

_____

_____

_____

For Further Study

1. Read Romans 7. What does Paul's struggle with the sin of covetousness tell us about how Christians are to respond to the law? What is his only hope and how does it speak Jesus' love to us?

_____

_____

_____

_____

2. Question 60 in *The Heidelberg Catechism* asks, "How are you righteous before God?" What is their answer? Respond. (I've included this question and answer in the endnotes in case you don't have a copy already.)[5]

_____

_____

_____

3. I'll leave you now with one last verse in which to find the law and the gospel: "Do not present your members to sin as instruments for unrighteousness, but present yourselves to God as those who have been brought from death to life" (Romans 6:13).

   a. Where is the law in this passage?

      _____

      _____

      _____

   b. Where is the gospel?

      _____

      _____

      _____

   c. How does remembering the gospel encourage you as you struggle to live a holy life?

      _____

      _____

      _____

8

Finding the Love of Jesus in the Gospel

For the law was given through Moses; grace and truth came through Jesus Christ.

John 1:17

We've come a long way together, haven't we? We've listened in as Jesus spoke words of love and assurance to many women. We've heard him claim that he is not only the author of the entire Old Testament but also its subject—a preposterous claim were it not spoken from lips that had just cried out, "Father, into your hands I commit my spirit!" (Luke 23:46). We've discovered that it was he working all throughout Israel's history, frequently as the angel of the Lord, leading his beloved yet disobedient children through their wilderness wanderings. We've seen the grace of God break through into the lives of distressed women like Eve, Hagar, Esther, Naomi, and Ruth. And we've seen him protect, pardon, and provide for a people who were waiting for their Messiah, though they would eventually crucify him. How could they have been so wrong about the very person they said they were longing for? They were that mistaken because they didn't know how to interpret their own Scriptures. They got the work and person of the Messiah all wrong. They put too much faith in their own ability to work their way into heaven and not enough faith in God's love for the whole world.

We, on the other hand, have been given the precious gift of Jesus' own post-resurrection proclamation: All of Moses' writings, the Psalms, and the Prophets were actually about him, his suffering, his glorification. Because we have that Emmaus road record, we can understand something the original audience couldn't: We can learn how the Old Testament is *not* to be read. It is not a map furnishing directions up a stairway into heaven, nor is it tea leaves that mysteriously reveal God's will from the bottom of your teacup. It's a proclamation of good news! It is the surprising announcement of God's plan to redeem a world that has thumbed its nose at him . . . and to do so at great personal cost.

We've learned that rather than the Old Testament being detached and in conflict with the New, it is the backdrop to the main attraction, the stage upon which the good news is acted out. We've seen that all narratives, letters, and prophecies in the New Testament find their origin in the Old.[1] The beautiful blossoms bursting from the New have their roots in and grow out of the ancient narrative that began: "In the beginning, God . . ." The message of Christ's work was actually declared throughout the Old Testament—sometimes in bold, headline type, and at other times in faint missives in the dark. But it is there nonetheless.

And now, finally, we've learned that the whole Bible is to be read with the understanding that it has two primary purposes.

The first is to tell us what God expects of us, what we're calling the law. The second shows us what God has already done for us, the gospel. Because these two functions are so different, wise women who study the Bible will strive to distinguish them and use each one as it should be used. To use the law as a ladder into heaven or the gospel as license to scoff at the law are equally foolish.

Finding the Gospel in the Story of Eve

Even at the very beginning of time, Jesus was speaking to us through the law and the gospel. See if you can find them both in this passage,

> The Lord God took the man and put him in the garden of Eden to work it and keep it. And the Lord God commanded the man saying, "You may surely eat of every tree of the garden, but of the tree of the knowledge of good and evil you shall not eat, for in the day that you eat of it you shall surely die."
>
> Genesis 2:15–17

Did you see both declarations and obligations (gospel and law) in those verses? Here are the declarations of God's kindness to Adam: He placed him in a beautiful garden, giving him good work to do, and filled the garden with delicious fruit for him to eat. The obligation in this passage is plain, too, isn't it? This is the law: "You shall not eat" from a certain tree, and if you do "you shall surely die."

Of course, you know the rest of the story. Satan, in the form of a serpent, tempted Eve to disobey God's good law, and after she did she shared her folly with her husband. They ate of the fruit that had been forbidden. Was there something poisonous in that fruit? I doubt it. It wasn't the fruit itself that was so dangerous for them to eat. It was the act of disobedience, of failing to trust in the goodness of the Lord, bringing upon themselves (and all of us) guilt and despair. They went from loving to walk with Jesus in the garden "in the cool of the day" to hiding behind a bush trying to cover their shame. The consciousness of a guilt that would bring death now hangs over every one of us.

Our DNA was infected with an awareness of coming doom. Instead of experiencing joyous self-forgetfulness and love for the Lord and others, Adam and Eve curved in on themselves and hid from God, knowing that destruction was their due. All their children (but One) would spend their lives trying to assuage or silence their guilty consciences by worshiping themselves and other gods. The death they "surely" experienced that day was the death of a guilt-free conscience and of unhindered, open, free fellowship with the Lord who was the Source and Sustainer of their lives. Their hearts were darkened. They forgot how to love. These psychological and spiritual deaths would, of course, eventuate in the death of their physical bodies. From that day on every unbeliever would live and die under the Curse of Death for Disobedience, "Cursed be anyone who does not confirm the words of this law by doing them" (Deuteronomy 27:26). And so death passed on to all people, even you and me.

This curse, called by Paul the "curse of the law," is what makes mankind hate the law and purpose to disobey it. It makes us sing stupid lyrics like *I did it my way!* Conversely, it functions as a relentless slave driver in the hearts of those who try (in vain) to justify themselves before God by it. The Curse of Death for Disobedience strips away the desire to obey and places us at odds with the Lord. Even believers who say, "I just can't do it (so I won't even try)!" are reaping the fruit of Eve's folly. Remember that obedience to the law is either pass or fail, perfection or destruction. But we all fail all the time. And so instead of the law being a welcome guide, sinners revolt against it. And even saints struggle to obey, which is why Paul wrote at the end of his confession of sin:

> Wretched man that I am! Who will deliver me from this body of death? Thanks be to God through Jesus Christ our Lord! . . . There is therefore now no condemnation for those who are in Christ Jesus.
>
> Romans 7:24–8:1

Did you hear Paul's lifesaving proclamation? He struggled to obey the law against coveting. But he found failure even when he tried to obey. His experience of wretchedness is the fruit of the Curse of Death for Disobedience. But Paul didn't remain in his wretchedness and neither did Eve. The Lord brought the answer to both of them: They will both be delivered from condemnation, their sentence of death for disobedience will be borne by Jesus Christ our Lord.

After her death-demanding sin, Eve heard the Lord's words of hope. Instead of "Off with her head!" she heard (in essence) in Genesis 3:15:

> I've got this. Your Son, who will also be my Son, will take all your punishment and bring you back here to me. I promise you all will be well again. Yes, our Son will be wounded, but he will crush our enemy. Live in the light of that promise and never despair. I am the Lord, your God.

Those words, sometimes called the *proto-evangelion* (first gospel), weren't spoken to Eve after she had properly repented and gotten her life back together. They came to her when she was crouching in shame in the shrubs and brought with them the hope that though her sin had shattered every relationship in her life, it couldn't completely destroy everything. Her sin wasn't powerful enough to overcome the world of love Jesus had created.

Barred from the Tree of Life

These words follow the Lord's proclamation of both judgment and eventual welcome:

> Then the Lord God said, "Behold the man has become like one of us in knowing good and evil. Now, lest he reach out his hand and take also of the tree of life and eat, and live forever—" therefore the Lord God sent him out from the garden of Eden . . . He drove out the man, and . . . placed the cherubim and a flaming sword that turned every way to guard the way to the tree of life.
>
> Genesis 3:22–24

Thankfully, our wretched parents were protected from remaining in their miserable state forever. They were barred from eating of the Tree of Life. They would eventually be delivered from this vale of tears, but their deliverance would come through death. Thus, the curse of death would come upon all people because the way to everlasting life was guarded by a sword-wielding cherubim. So even though death is a grievous part of the curse for disobedience (and grievous it is), it is also a sweet relief from our wretchedness.

Welcomed to the Tree of Life . . . Then, Now, and in Eternity

But, of course, this isn't the end of our mother's story. The gospel tells us of another tree, a cursed one. And here again we see Jesus doing what he's always done: providing for us, protecting and pardoning us. Here we see the only human who lived a life of *perfect* obedience, free from the Curse of Death for Disobedience, willingly hanging in disgrace and wretchedness in our place. Are you ready for the best news ever? "Christ redeemed us from the curse of the law [death for disobedience] by becoming a curse for us—for it is written, 'Cursed is everyone who is hanged on a tree'" (Galatians 3:13).

He became the cursed One so we could go free. Notice that a sword is thrust into his side. . . . Could this be that sword that was tasked with keeping us from the Tree of Life?

The Curse of Death for Disobedience that we all live under is meant to continually force our eyes away from ourselves, away from our deadly doing, away from our rebellion, to Calvary. Like the first use of the law, it is meant to crush us and bring us back to the One with whom we are invited to walk in the cool of the day. There he is, our Lord Jesus, bearing in his body all the condemnation we deserve so that we never have to face a sentence of eternal death. This is the gospel, and here it is in the beginning of the Bible.

But that is not the last time we hear about a Tree of Life. A day will come when all believers will be invited to eat freely from it on the New Earth. Read and believe that this day is coming:

> Then the angel showed me the river of the water of life, bright as crystal, flowing from the throne of God and of the Lamb through the middle of the street of the city; also, on either side of the river, the tree of life with its twelve kinds of fruit, yielding its fruit each month. The leaves of the tree were for the healing of the nations. No longer will there be anything accursed.
>
> Revelation 22:1–3

Notice that nothing cursed will be there. The curse will be completely gone. Glorious day!

Can you see how the message of the gospel has been preached throughout the entire history of the world? Isn't that wonderful news?

Finding His Love in Sarah's Story

About one thousand years after that first gospel message was delivered, the angel of the Lord (you know who this is) visited Abram (Abraham) and his wife, Sarai (Sarah) by an oak grove. Abram had already believed the absurd promise that his infertile wife would mother a son who would bring blessing to "all the families of the earth" (Genesis 12:3). But decades had passed, and aside from that mistake with Hagar and Ishmael, no promised sons were anywhere to be seen. In addition, Abraham was more than one hundred years old, and Sarah was ninety—not exactly prime childbearing ages, no matter when you lived.

Then, on one ordinary hot desert day, while Abraham sat by the door of his tent and Sarah worked inside, Jesus came calling (see Genesis 18). He said, "I will surely return to you about this time next year, and Sarah your wife will have a son" (v. 10). A muffled laugh crackled forth from Sarah's aged lungs. "After I am worn out, and my lord is old, shall I have pleasure?" (v. 12). Jesus' response to her comical hopelessness was "Why did Sarah laugh . . . ? Is anything too hard for the Lord?" Her response? "I did not laugh." Jesus said, "But you did laugh" (vv. 13–15), *but that's not going to stop me from blessing you.*

You know the rest of the story: "The Lord visited Sarah as he had said, and the Lord did to Sarah as he had promised. And Sarah conceived and bore Abraham a son in his old age" (Genesis 21:1–2). The scheming, cynical, laughing, lying old woman of nearly invisible faith received the promise of blessing and is called a holy woman and the "mother" of every other believing woman (1 Peter 3:6). Even the writer of Hebrews shines up her reputation by saying, "She considered him faithful who had promised" (Hebrews 11:11). Did Sarah earn this blessing by obeying the law? Of course not! Sarah was chosen as an instrument of grace; she was the perfect example of a woman who didn't deserve blessings and yet lived out her days rejoicing in Isaac, her son of laughter, because of God's love. But this isn't just a "and they lived happily ever after" story disconnected from you and me. No, it's all about us. Paul writes that Jesus bore the curse in our place "so that in Christ Jesus the blessing of Abraham might come to the Gentiles, so that we might receive the promised Spirit through faith" (Galatians 3:14).

The promised blessing and freedom from the curse, through the power of the life-giving Spirit, has already been bestowed on us. All the promises of relationship, freedom, and happiness have been given to us as daughters of a very weak and flawed woman who lied and whose mouth was filled with holy laughter by a gracious loving Lord.

The Gospel Tells Us How to Be Right with God

Hundreds of years ago, godly men sought to lay out, in very plain terms, the gospel message. The way they did it was by asking and then answering this question: "How are you righteous with God?" Here's their answer:

> Only by a true faith in Jesus Christ; that is, though my conscience accuse me, that I have grievously sinned against all the

commandments of God and kept none of them, and am still inclined to all evil, yet God, without any merit of mine, of mere grace, grants and imputes to me the perfect satisfaction, righteousness, and holiness of Christ, as if I had never had nor committed any sin, and myself had accomplished all the obedience which Christ has rendered for me; if only I accept such benefit with a believing heart.[2]

Isn't that the best news you've ever heard? While it is true that our conscience accuses us with grievously breaking the law and of actually still wanting to, by his grace God "grants and imputes" to us all that Jesus did for us. He looks at us as though we had never sinned, but also as though we had been perfectly obedient. That wretched state of being cursed by disobedience has been *completely* and *forever* obliterated by grace! And if we will simply receive this truth and believe that God is too good to lie to us, he will count us as fully justified. Simply, justification means: just as if I had never sinned *and* just as if I had always obeyed.

What? Me? Us? *Never* sinned? *Always* obeyed? Here's what Paul had to say:

- "For there is no distinction: for all have sinned and fall short of the glory of God, and are justified by his grace as a gift, through the redemption that is in Christ Jesus . . . to be received by faith" (Romans 3:22–25).
- "For we hold that one is justified by faith apart from the works of the law" (Romans 3:28).
- "Therefore, since we have been justified by faith, we have peace with God through our Lord Jesus Christ" (Romans 5:1).
- "For with the heart one believes and is justified" (Romans 10:10).

Where does this faith to believe and be justified come from? The Lord, of course. The Lord who has been providing for us, protecting and pardoning us all along, is also providing faith to believe to women who are dead and unable to do so. Faith is a gift granted to us by God's grace: "For by grace you have been saved through faith. And this is not your own doing; it is the gift of God" (Ephesians 2:8).

May God be praised forever!

Back to Sunday School on the Road to Emmaus

We've taken quite a journey, haven't we? We started out eavesdropping on a conversation between a nephew and his aunt and uncle as they journeyed away from the place of his execution and resurrection. We've seen how he claimed to be the writer of all their Scriptures and how every part of it, from narratives, to prophecy, to songs and sayings, were signposts proclaiming his loving plan of redemption for the whole world. We've seen how it is just as easy for us to misread it as it was for his original audience—and the dreadful results of doing so. And finally we've learned that the entire Bible, both Old and New Testaments, can be divided into two categories: *law* and *gospel*, and how we're to respond to each one differently.

Learning to read the whole Bible in this way, searching for Jesus, listening to the proclamations of the law and the gospel, will enrich and motivate us to spend time reading, anticipating the joy of discovery. Our study will become more than dry duty, moral injunctions, or ancient predictions of happenings in some far-off land. Rather, it will build our faith and bring us hope that every facet of our lives, including the times in which we live, are all part of God's gracious plan to acquaint us with

Jesus, the Man who has always loved us. It will enable us to see *one grand design* being played out over thousands of years and awaiting its climax in the return and rebuilding of the world once marred by our sin.

Right now, I am praying that each one of you will make this your goal as you read: "Do your best to present yourself to God as one approved, a worker who has no need to be ashamed, rightly handling the word of truth" (2 Timothy 2:15).

You have been forgiven, loved, welcomed, and freed from the Curse of Death for Disobedience. You've been given the Holy Spirit, whose job it is to open your eyes to Jesus' person and work. So now, with confidence and courage, you can begin to read again, asking Jesus to show you how everything written in the books of Moses, the Psalms, and the Prophets are about his suffering and glory. You are his beloved daughter. He has been loving you throughout all eternity, and now that you know how to find him, you can enjoy his words of love to you.

Open Bible, Open Heart

1. Recount the gospel according to Eve. Respond.

_____

_____

_____

_____

2. Recount the gospel according to Sarah. Respond.

_____

_____

_____

_____

_____

3. Reread the question and answer about being right with God on pages 141–142 (*The Heidelberg Catechism* Q & A 60). Respond.

_____

_____

_____

_____

_____

4. What have you learned about "rightly handling the word of truth" (2 Timothy 2:15) from our time together?

_____

_____

_____

_____

_____

5. In four or five sentences, summarize what you've learned in this chapter.

_____

_____

_____

_____

_____

6. Go back and review all the summary sentences at the end of every chapter and summarize them. What two or three truths are you going to take from this study and use in your Bible reading?

_____

_____

_____

_____

_____

FOR FURTHER STUDY

1. Find a copy of *The Heidelberg Catechism*—the one I use has study notes—and spend time reading and praying about question and answer 60 (also included in this chapter on pages 141–142). Write out verses that make the glorious truth of the gospel more precious to you and keep them in your Bible, so when you start reading, you can remember that you are loved.[3]

Appendix

Coming to Saving Faith

Welcome. I'm glad you're here, because I have some really amazing news for you. This news is actually so amazing, so *good*, that the people who lived when it was first being talked about called it the *good* news or the *gospel*. You've probably heard that term *gospel* before and might have wondered about it. When Christians are using it, it really does mean "good news," and in particular, good news of a certain sort.

So, what's the good news and what does it have to do with "saving faith"? First of all, it is news. Think of a news story you read on your computer or hear on the nightly news. News is generally thought of as a story about actual events. But unlike the daily news feed on our phones, the gospel is about events that happened thousands of years ago in the Middle East.

This story starts out with a husband and his wife, in fact, the first people who ever lived. The Lord, their loving Father, placed them in a very beautiful garden; he had given them life and everything they needed to be completely happy. But one day Satan, a creature that hated both them and their Father, tricked them into disobeying their Father. This disobedience brought sadness and death to them and to all of us, as the Lord said it would.

In disobeying the Lord, they transformed from people who were capable of sinning into people who sinned because it was their nature. They began to die. Their bodies began to degenerate and, saddest of all, their relationship with the Lord and with each other began to die also. The Lord exiled the man and woman from their beautiful garden home, but before they left, he gave them a promise: Someday a Son will be born who will crush this Enemy and make everything right again. Yes, they had to leave their home, but their Father promised them that someday they would be able to return.

Thousands of years passed, and after God had accomplished many things through his people Israel, the world was finally ready to receive the One he had promised.

About two thousand years ago, a young virgin girl from Israel was visited by God. She was told that she would be the one who would bear the longed-for Messiah, the Promised One. Her name was Mary. By a miraculous act of God through the Holy Spirit, she became pregnant with the Son, the second person of the Trinity. The Messiah's birth had to happen like this because, though a human being was necessary to complete God's work, only God could actually accomplish it. The Promised One had to be both man and God at the same time. The Father needed to send someone to his people who would obey all his commands and never sin, but yet be willing and able to bear the punishment of death for our disobedience. The girl's child was named *Jesus*, which means "God saves!" and he was the Christ, or the Messiah, the Promised One. He was the One for whom the Jewish people had been longing for thousands of years. Jesus was Mary's son, but he was also God's Son.

Jesus grew up in an ordinary Jewish home, but in one way he was very different from everyone else. He never sinned. Another way to say that is to say that he perfectly loved his Father with his whole heart, soul, mind, and strength, and he always loved his neighbor the same way he loved himself.

You would think that a person who was so loving would be really popular, wouldn't you? And while there was a time when he really did have a lot of friends, there were also other people who were jealous of him and of the fact that he was getting more popular than they were. They also hated him because he called them out about their sin and hypocrisy. So they decided to shut him up and, of course, the best way to do that permanently was to kill him.

One day, they talked their corrupt rulers into conspiring with them, and eventually they killed him. That happened on a day we now strangely call Good Friday. Jesus, the man who always loved everyone, was laughed at while he was being executed on a cross. He died in exile, even from his Father. He was standing in the place of every person who had ever sinned; he was being punished and exiled for them. And he was imputing or transferring to them his record of never sinning, of always loving his Father and his neighbor.

While all of this might seem like really bad news, the truth is that everything was going according to God's plan. Remember how he gave his promise to send someone who would defeat Satan, the one who had tricked the first man and woman? This was how he accomplished that. In that ancient prophecy, God said that the Rescuer would crush the Enemy, but he also said that the Enemy would strike the Rescuer.

After Jesus died, some of his followers took his lifeless body down from the cross and carried it to a cave in a garden. The jealous religious leaders were afraid people might steal his body and say that he hadn't died after all, so they had soldiers roll a large stone in front of the cave where his body had been laid. Then a group of them were stationed by the cave as guards to make sure there would be no trickery going on.

But . . . God had a different plan. On the third morning, Jesus' Father declared that his Son had completed everything he had sent him to do, and so he raised his body from the dead. We celebrate that day on Easter. Easter proves that Jesus was who he said he was and that he accomplished everything his Father had sent him to do. It proves that he is God.

After his resurrection, Jesus was seen by hundreds of people, many of whom died because they wouldn't change their story and say that he was still dead. They were completely convinced, and because of that they were willing to suffer in terrible ways.

You might be wondering how this story is good news and what it has to do with you. I understand. Here's why it is good news: The truth is that you and I, all people in fact, are sinners. We all fail to love God and our neighbor. Sometimes we fail to love in little ways, like being angry at someone because our coffee isn't exactly the way we like it. Other times we fail to love in really big ways, like lying or stealing or even committing adultery. No matter how we fail, we all fail to love *all the time*. And none of us puts God first in our lives like we should. In fact, we don't even live up to our own standards most of the time. Because we are sinners, we have the sentence of death hanging over us. God promised that all who sin will die (Romans 6:23).

The good news is that all the punishment you and I deserve for all the sin we have committed was poured out on Jesus. That's why he died. That means the punishment of death for disobedience no longer applies to those who believe in Jesus' sacrifice for them. But that's not all the good news there is. The next part of the good news is that the whole record of all the love that Jesus showed to his Father and to all people is ours. We are forgiven for all our sins *and* we have Jesus' perfect record besides! Amazing, yes? That's what the Bible means when it says we are justified. Justification means two things. First of all, it means that as far as God is concerned, when he looks at us it is just as if we had never sinned. Second, it also means that when he looks at us it is just as if we had always obeyed. Because of the work of Jesus, those who believe on him are both completely forgiven and made completely righteous.

But there is more good news. We are not only forgiven and counted obedient, God also welcomes us back into his Home in heaven. You remember that the first couple was exiled out of their beautiful garden because they disobeyed God. Well, the great news is that Jesus has reopened the gates to that garden for us and is welcoming us back Home.

You might be wondering what you have to do to get rid of that death sentence, get a perfect record, and procure an invitation into God's house. The really great news is this: *All you have to do is believe.* Really. Just believe. Believe that the story I've just told you is true and then put your trust in Jesus, his life, death, and resurrection, and all that I've just said will be true for you. It's called "saving faith," which simply means this: You believe you have sinned and need a Savior, and you believe that Jesus is the Savior you need. And you are saved. Period.

Now, of course, if you believe this is true, you'll want to be around other people who believe this, too, and you'll want to learn more about it. You need to find a Bible-believing church and become a part of it. That's why I have gone to church almost every Sunday for the forty-plus years since I first believed. No church is perfect. It's a place that is full of people just like you and me, sinners who need a Savior. But church is the place where God has promised to meet us. Look for a church near you that has a statement of faith that you can read, and see if it declares the same story I just told you. (Mormons and Jehovah's Witnesses are not Christians.)

The next thing you should do is get a Bible, or go online and find one that is available to read for free. I really like the translation called the English Standard Version (used in this book), but there are other good ones, as well. You might want to start reading in the New Testament, which is the part of the Bible that starts with the stories about Jesus and the books called the Gospels. And, of course, you'll want to start praying—talking to your Father God, and to Jesus, your Brother. They will love to hear from you, and will answer your prayers in the way that is best for you.

Does this sound too good to be true? I know. It really is amazing. That's why they call it the good news! But if you sense God is calling you to come to him, just put your faith and trust in him and in his Word. Believe in him, that he is loving and good and wise, and has great things in store for you.

If you have come to faith through reading this book, I'd really like to know. You can contact me through the publisher or my website, www.elysefitzpatrick.com. Thanks!

Now it's time for you to turn back to the front of this book and start reading about how to understand the great book God has given to us: the Bible.

Notes

Introduction: Forever and Forever He Has Loved Us

1. 2 Timothy 1:9.

2. In this book, as we look closely at that love, don't forget that it's the Trinity—Father, Son, and Spirit—who love you like this.

3. The Greek is normally rendered in English *Rabboni*, which in this diminutive form of the term does not imply "little" but rather a term of acknowledging personally the honor due the rabbi, such as "my beloved rabbi" or "my dear rabbi." See Bauer, Arndt, Gingrich, and Danker, *Greek-English Lexicon of the New Testament*, 733, and W. F. Albright, "Recent Discoveries in Palestine and Jerusalem" in *The Background of the New Testament and Its Eschatology* (Cambridge, UK: Clarendon Press, 1956), 158.

4. Dr. James Boice, "Who Were the Disciples on the Road to Emmaus?," http://www.jesus.org/death-and-resurrection/resurrection/who-were-the-disciples-on-the-road-to-emmaus.html.

5. Although I'm convinced that the second disciple is his aunt Mary, you might not be. I enjoy the thought of Jesus speaking with his aunt, a woman who had loved and supported him in his ministry, and who was undoubtedly shattered by his death. But if you would rather think it's not the case, it doesn't diminish the importance of the truth that he taught them.

Chapter 1: It's All about Him

1. Barna Research Group, *Barna Trends: What's New and What's Next at the Intersection of Faith and Culture* (Grand Rapids, MI: Baker Books, 2016), 140.

2. "To release or set free, with the implied analogy to the process of freeing a slave—'to set free, to liberate, to deliver, liberation, deliverance.'"

λυτρόομαι: ἡμεῖς δὲ ἠλπίζομεν ὅτι αὐτός ἐστιν ὁ μέλλων λυτροῦσθαι τὸν Ἰσραήλ: "But we had hoped that he was the one to redeem Israel" (Luke 24:21). Johannes P. Louw and Eugene Albert Nida, *Greek-English Lexicon of the New Testament: Based on Semantic Domains* (New York: United Bible Societies, 1996), 487.

3. Matt. 16:21; 17:23; 20:19; Mark 8:31; 10:34; Luke 9:22; 18:33; 24:6–7; John 2:19.

4. *ESV Study Bible* (Wheaton, IL: Crossway, 2008), note on Luke 24:27.

Chapter 2: Seeing What's Right before You

1. Louw and Nida, *Greek-English Lexicon of the New Testament: Based on Semantic Domains*, 385–86.

2. Dennis E Johnson, *Walking With Jesus Through His Word* (Phillipsburg, NJ: P & R Publishing, 2015), 19.

3. The *ESV Reformation Study Bible* lists 343 exact quotations from the Old Testament to the New (Wheaton, IL: Crossway, 2011), 2608–11.

Chapter 3: Finding the Love of Jesus in the Books of Moses

1. Because the end of Deuteronomy records Moses' death, it is assumed that someone else, perhaps Joshua, finished his writings.

2. *ESV Study Bible* (Wheaton, IL: Crossway, 2008), *How the New Testament Quotes and Interprets the Old Testament*, 2607.

3. For ease of communication, I'm going to take the liberty of referring to the preincarnate Son as Jesus from now on, though he didn't assume that name until after his incarnation and birth.

4. The connection between the angel of the Lord and the preincarnate appearance of the Messiah cannot be denied. (A. Bowling, TWOT 1:464–65; G. B. Funderburk, ZPEB 1:160–66; J. B. Payne, *Theology of the Older Testament*, http://www.biblestudytools.com/dictionaries/bakers-evangelical-dictionary /angel-of-the-lord.html).

5. Instances where we might assume that the angel of the Lord is a theophany include Gen. 16:7–13; 22:11–18; 31:11–13; Num. 22:22–23; Judges 2:1–4; 5:23; 6:11–16; 13:3, 13–22; Zech. 3:1–6. A theophany is an "appearance or manifestation of God; a compound word derived from the Greek noun for God and the Greek verb *to appear*." Walter A. Elwell and Barry J. Beitzel, "Theophany," *Baker Encyclopedia of the Bible* (Grand Rapids, MI: Baker Book House, 1988), 2050.

6. There are, however, times when the angel of the Lord has a conversation with another person referred to as "the Lord," and in those times we shouldn't assume that it's Jesus come with a message to his people. (See 2 Sam. 24:16 and Zech. 1:11–13.)

7. She named the place where she met him *Beer-lahai-roi*, which means "well of the Living One, who sees me" (*ESV Study Bible*, note on Genesis 16:14, 79).

8. *ESV Gospel Transformation Bible* (Wheaton, IL: Crossway, 2013), note on 1 Cor. 10:1–22, 1,541.

9. Paul, too, wrote that "Christ, our Passover lamb, has been sacrificed" (1 Cor. 5:7).

Chapter 4: Finding the Love of Jesus in Israel's Stories

1. The other place where this genre is employed is in the New Testament, in the Gospels and in the book of Acts.

2. *ESV Gospel Transformation Bible*, note on Psa. 83:9, 731.

3. "The Lord routed Sisera and all his chariots and all his army before Barak" (Judges 4:14–15). Who was it that "routed" Sisera that day? The Lord Jesus, of course. How do we know? Because the apostle Paul applied an obscure verse David had written about this battle directly to him. In Ephesians 4:8, he identified that conquering King as ultimately referring to the resurrected Jesus: "When he ascended on high he led a host of captives, and he gave gifts to men."

4. *ESV Gospel Transformation Bible*, study note on Judges 4:12–16, 306.

5. Iain M. Duguid, *Esther and Ruth: Reformed Expository Commentary* (Phillipsburg, NJ: P & R Publishing, 2005), 130.

6. Elyse Fitzpatrick, notes on Esther, *ESV Gospel Transformation Bible*, 599.

7. Ibid., 606.

8. Ibid., 605.

9. Ibid.

10. Ibid., 608.

Chapter 5: Finding the Love of Jesus in His Songs and Sayings

1. I've actually heard people say that the reason Job suffered was because he didn't have strong enough faith. Aside from the audacity that would cause someone to think their faith was perfect enough to pass muster, you'd have to ignore the entire beginning and end of the book to conclude that Job was being punished for unbelief. This is the kind of Scripture twisting that brings despair to sufferers and is the result of reading the Bible like a moralist, searching for a moral lesson to be embraced so that one might avoid suffering and earn blessing.

2. C. S. Lewis, *The Lion, the Witch and the Wardrobe* (New York: Harper-Collins, 2008), 163.

3. Matt. 21:16, 42; Luke 6:3–4.

4. "Twenty-eight Prophecies Fulfilled on the Crucifixion Day," https://www .cbcg.org/franklin/SA/SA_28prophecies.pdf.

5. *ESV Gospel Transformation Bible*, 793.

6. Matt. 9:12–13; Luke 7:36ff; Matt. 15:21ff; 9:20ff; Rom. 5:6, 8; John 4:1–26.

7. *ESV Gospel Transformation Bible*, 835.

8. Iain M. Duguid, *The Song of Songs: Tyndale Old Testament Commentaries* (Downers Grove, IL: InterVarsity Press, 2015), 51.

Chapter 6: Finding the Love of Jesus in His Prophets

1. The English Standard Version Study Bible is a great example of this. It furnishes both a formal "Introduction to the Prophetic Books" as well as introductions to specific books like Isaiah and Jeremiah. Then the notes attached to verses, as well as the headings at chapters and paragraphs, will also help you know what the words meant to those who first heard and read them. You don't

need to be a Bible scholar to be able to understand what the prophets were originally talking about; thankfully, most of that work has already been done for you by people who are.

2. In Matthew's Gospel alone he wrote that the events surrounding Jesus fulfilled prophecy no less than fifteen times.

3. Some of the connections they made were surprising. In fact, if we didn't know that the New Testament was inspired by the Holy Spirit, we might wonder whether these "infallible interpreters" weren't stretching the connections a bit too far.

4. "Some of the most important prophecies about Christ accurately predicted His birthplace (Mic. 5:2), flight to Egypt (Hos. 11:1), the identity of His forerunner (Mal. 3:1), His entering Jerusalem on a donkey (Zech. 9:9), betrayal for thirty pieces of silver (Zech. 11:12), humiliation and beating (Isa. 50:6), crucifixion with other prisoners (Isa. 53:12), hand and feet wounds (Ps. 22:16), side wound (Zech. 12:10), soldiers gambling for His clothing (Ps. 22:18), His burial in a rich man's tomb (Isa. 53:9), resurrection (Ps. 16:10; 49:15), and second coming (Ps. 50:3–6; Isa. 9:6–7; Dan. 7:13–14; Zech. 14:4–8)." Dan Story, *Defending Your Faith* (Grand Rapids, MI: Kregel Publications, 1997), 78.

5. In a book entitled *Science Speaks*, Peter W. Stoner claimed that 10^{17} "silver dollars would be enough to cover the face of the entire state of Texas two feet deep. Now, I've been to Texas. I've driven for days to get across Texas. Texas is a very big state. Who in his right mind would suppose that a blindfolded man, heading out of Dallas by foot in any direction, would be able, on his very first attempt, to pick up one specifically marked silver dollar out of 100,000,000,000,000,000?," http://www.christiananswers.net/q-aiia/jesus-odds.html. See Peter W Stoner, *Science Speaks: Scientific Proof of the Accuracy of Prophecy and the Bible* (Chicago: Moody Press), 1969.

6. Prophecies are also frequently given in poetic and allegorical language, so we should not read them as if they were in the same genre as the history or law books.

7. *ESV Gospel Transformation Bible*, 1121.

8. Hosea, Joel, Amos, Obadiah, Jonah, Micah, Nahum, Habakkuk, Zephaniah, Haggai, Zechariah, and Malachi.

9. They range in length from one chapter (Obadiah) to fourteen (Hosea and Zechariah).

10. *ESV Gospel Transformation Bible*, note on Zechariah 3:1–10, 1244.

11. *ESV Gospel Transformation Bible*, note on Daniel 7:9–12, 1135.

Chapter 7: Finding the Love of Jesus in His Law

1. Do we need to love ourselves? Let's take a little side excursion for a moment to clear up some confusion about loving God, our neighbor, and ourselves. I know many people say we are commanded to love ourselves and that we can't love God or our neighbor well until we excel at loving ourselves. People tell us that we need to love ourselves more, when the truth is just the opposite: We already love ourselves too much. There's a saying in Latin, *incurvatus in se*,

which describes this problem. It means that we are "curved in on ourselves." Unless we're making a conscious effort to love God and our neighbor, we *always* choose to love ourselves first. It's in our DNA. It's part of our sin nature. God never commands us to love ourselves. He doesn't have to because we already do. When Jesus said that we are to love our neighbor as ourselves, he wasn't commanding us to love ourselves. He was assuming that we already did, which was what was stopping us from loving others.

I admit that if I were commanded to love myself, I could obey. I love myself by nature. Even on the days when I "hate" myself for all the stupid things I am, say, or do, I only hate myself because I can't believe that the one person I love more than anyone else is such a loser. All of my self-hatred is actually driven by a deep self-love. If I really hated myself, I wouldn't care about who or what I am. Like everyone else, I have a terminal case of *incurvatus in se.*

2. Augustine wrote, "The law bids us, as we try to fulfill its requirements, and become wearied in our weakness under it, to know how to ask the help of grace." http://www.ligonier.org/blog/threefold-use-law/.

3. *Groundhog Day* (Columbia Pictures Industries, Inc., 1993).

4. See the Formula of Concord (VI. The Third Use of the Law); *Heidelberg Catechism*, Question and Answer 86; http://www.ligonier.org/blog/threefold -use-law/; Calvin's Institutes 2.7.12

5. *Heidelberg Catechism*, Question and Answer 60:

Q: How are you righteous before God?

A: Only by true faith in Jesus Christ. Although my conscience accuses me that I have grievously sinned against all God's commandments, have never kept any of them, and am still inclined to all evil, yet God, without any merit of my own, out of mere grace, imputes to me the perfect satisfaction, righteousness, and holiness of Christ. He grants these to me as if I had never had nor committed any sin, and as if I myself had accomplished all the obedience which Christ has rendered for me, if only I accept this gift with a believing heart.

Chapter 8: Finding the Love of Jesus in the Gospel

1. I've heard it said that the New Testament is the inspired commentary on the Old.

2. G. I. Williamson, *The Heidelberg Catechism: A Study Guide* (Phillipsburg, NJ: P & R Publishing, 1993), Question 60, 106.

3. Williamson, *The Heidelberg Catechism: A Study Guide*, 1993.

Elyse Fitzpatrick is a nationally sought-after speaker and author, speaking at such events as The Gospel Coalition and Nancy Leigh DeMoss Wolgemuth's Revive Conference. Along with her husband, Phil, Elyse is a member of Valley Center Community Church, a reformed congregation in the community of Valley Center. VCCC is a member of FIRE, the Fellowship of Independent Reformed Evangelicals.

She holds a certificate in Biblical Counseling from Christian Counseling & Educational Foundation (CCEF), San Diego, and an MA in Biblical Counseling from Trinity Theological Seminary. She has authored twenty-three books on daily living and the Christian life.

Elyse has been married for more than forty years and has three adult children and six grandchildren. Learn more at www.elyse fitzpatrick.com.

More from Elyse Fitzpatrick

Visit elysefitzpatrick.com for a full list of her books.

This world is not our home, and deep down we all feel a longing to find the place we truly belong. Exploring heaven and the afterlife, Elyse Fitzpatrick gives you a glimpse of your eternal home, the New Earth. It's not a dull space in the clouds but rather a perfected earth—a wondrous, physical place to explore and enjoy an eternity with God.

Home

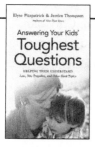

It can be hard to know what to say when your kids ask questions about difficult topics, from death to the devil to the latest tragedy on the news. How much should you say—and when? This unique guide walks you through these conversations, offering practical insight and guidance.

Answering Your Kids' Toughest Questions
by Elyse Fitzpatrick and Jessica Thompson